DÎNER À LA MAISON

DÎNER À LA MAISON

A Parisian's Guide to Cooking and Entertaining at Home

LAURENT BUTTAZZONI

INTRODUCTION BY SOFIA COPPOLA

Photography by Charlotte Hess

with Aude Buttazzoni

RIZZOLI
NEW YORK

New York · Paris · London · Milan

TABLE OF CONTENTS

Introduction by Sofia Coppola **7**

Foreword by Laurent Buttazzoni **9**

A Parisian's Guide to Cooking and Entertaining at Home **10**

WEEKDAY MENUS

Baked sea bass; broccoli, avocado, fennel, and cilantro salad **17**

Veal burgers; warm smoky sautéed mushrooms; fresh herb salad **21**

Marinated chicken; Caesar Salad; strawberry and pistachio ice cream **25**

Linguine with Genovese pesto **29**

Oven-roasted salmon; potato salad; raw and cooked beet salad; cucumbers with yogurt **33**

Roast rack of lamb with pan juices; green tabbouleh **37**

Skate with caper–lemon zest gremolata; three-tomato salad **41**

Fusilli with sausage **45**

Cod with cilantro pesto; watercress salad with mushrooms, cucumbers, and avocado; berry trifle **49**

Watercress soup; French mac 'n' cheese **55**

Risotto primavera; French bean salad **59**

Monkfish stew; grated carrots and zucchini salad; warm quinoa salad **63**

Pumpkin soup; roast veal; herby mashed potatoes **67**

Gem lettuce with anchovies; linguine with prawns and arugula **73**

Caponata; soft-boiled eggs **77**

Smoked haddock chowder; open-faced avocado tartines **81**

Leek "maki"; pork tonkatsu; crunchy coleslaw **85**

Zucchini with mint and pine nuts; calamari, chickpeas, and chorizo; sgroppino **89**

Lemon-scented veal scallopini; braised artichokes **95**

Treviso salad with anchovies; octopus, potatoes, and pimentón; espresso affogato **99**

Creamy celeriac soup with sage butter; scallops; haricot beans **105**

WEEKEND AND HOLIDAY MENUS

Leeks mimosa with vinaigrette; veal stew in tomato sauce **113**

Pasta alla Norma **117**

Roasted green asparagus; summer osso bucco **121**

Creamy bell pepper soup; salad Niçoise; Neapolitan ricotta cake **125**

Saffron-scented risotto with mussels; orange salad with fennel **131**

Belgian endive salad with pears and blue cheese; duck breast à l'orange; honey-glazed turnips **135**

Asparagus vichyssoise; vitello tonnato **141**

Fennel and mushroom salad with parmigiano reggiano; provençal braised beef stew;
     vanilla ice cream with olive oil and fleur de sel **147**

Tagliatelle al ragù; crunchy mixed vegetable salad **155**

Poule au pot; poached vegetables **157**

Tortellini in broth; chicken terrine aspic with green sauce **163**

Roast leg of lamb; cauliflower and potato curry (aloo gobi); radish salad **167**

Shepherd's pie of confit duck; sautéed mixed greens **171**

Mackerel fillets; middle eastern carrots; frozen yogurt with Turkish Delight and pistachios **177**

Watermelon, feta, and kalamata olive salad; sausages with lentils **183**

My Grandmother's braised rabbit; polenta fries; baked apples **187**

Mussels with semolina, scented with garlic, ginger, and cilantro **193**

Baby spinach salad with pomegranate seeds; slow cooked and roasted lemon and garlic chicken;
     bulgur with cilantro **197**

Mercedes chili beans; guacamole; margaritas **203**

Breakfast: A pair of ceviches; slow-cooked bonito salad with haricot beans; Mimosa cocktails **209**

Christmas time party: foie gras on endive leaves; oysters on the half shell;
     lentils with grilled sausages **219**

Acknowledgments **222**

Credits **223**

INTRODUCTION
BY SOFIA COPPOLA

I first I met the architect, Laurent Buttazzoni, when I was in Paris filming *Marie-Antoinette*. He and his partner, Robert Ferrell, hosted me and my crew for great dinners and fun barbeques at their beautiful home with friends.

In the years since then, I have had so many memorable dinners at their places in Paris and in Sicily and wish I could entertain like that. Laurent sets the greatest looking table settings and the food is always chic and delicious and easy, never fussy.

What started as me asking them for recipes here and there, and to send pictures of their place settings, has turned into this book that I've wanted and that I want to be able to share with friends.

I hope you enjoy with the people you love!

FOREWORD
BY LAURENT BUTTAZZONI

For Sofia and Robert, for their love and belief.

I love food and I love cooking for friends. It was my grandmothers who taught me to appreciate great ingredients and how to entertain at home in an accessible way. One was French, the other Italian-Hungarian; they both had chickens and rabbits and a vegetable garden in the yard. One cooked in a classic French style—riz au lait and poireaux-vinaigrette. The other was altogether more exotic—she made her gnocchi by hand and grew arugula in her garden long before anyone in France had ever heard of the salad. I would watch and taste and help in my grandmothers' kitchens and in their gardens. That is how I learned to cook: by looking and tasting.

Then I grew up and moved to Paris. I became an interior architect. I spent my days trying to bring beauty and elegance into the homes of my clients. I met Robert and, after a few years, we moved in together. We shared and still share a love of entertaining at home. We've had so many parties and dinners over the years: the Red birthday party, the World Cup party, the Caviar party... We've had chili buffets for thirty and candlelit dinners for six. We love to fill our home with our friends and we love to make them happy and feel appreciated when they are with us.

It was Sofia Coppola who suggested I write a book. But my days were always too busy with interior projects. A couple of years ago, my health gave me cause to re-evaluate my life, and during the hiatus of that time I realized what I really wanted to do more than anything else was to write the book that Sofia had suggested.

I hope that *Dîner à la Maison* becomes your friend in the kitchen. I hope I can show you how to cook delicious food and entertain at home simply and elegantly, whatever your budget. I want to take away the intimidation of having people over. I want to show you how to have the "wow factor" without the anxiety.

I would like *Dîner à la Maison* to bring pleasure into your everyday life, to inspire you for your big parties, and to be there for your intimate dinners.

Let's entertain together.

A PARISIAN'S GUIDE TO COOKING AND ENTERTAINING AT HOME
BY LAURENT BUTTAZZONI

Funnily enough, while I remember very well the first dinner I ever gave in honor of a couple of dear friends—Daniel and Maria Luisa Poumaillou—I cannot remember the menu. The rest of the scene remains very clear in my memory: One of my first apartments near Père Lachaise; a very low, white, square table in minimal and white surroundings; white Ikea plates, white bistro cutlery, balloon glasses; no tablecloth, but beautiful damask cloth napkins I had bought at the last moment—it was inconceivable to me to receive with paper towels. You need to start somewhere!

The white Ikea service accompanied me for a few years, until the day I decided it was finally time to acquire a porcelain service. So again I chose white, a classic impeccable design, and I use it virtually every day. This is the basis for all future variations: the equivalent of a beautiful white shirt in your wardrobe. (Choose a style that, in the event you break something, will allow you to replace it.)

The same rule applies to cutlery: keep a simple, timeless set in stainless steel, or—by looking for very nice pieces in silver—even a mismatched collection can make up a lovely service. Glasses lend themselves to more fantasy because they can be found for all budgets and in all shapes and colors. I always keep clear, transparent glasses for wine and patterned or colored ones for water.

On the other hand you can really have fun with textiles, and I often look for colorful placemats in washable and reusable fabrics. A set of placemats is of course a much less tedious alternative to a tablecloth, which must be washed, ironed, and stored. Travel is an unending source of supply and inspiration to find interesting fabrics—I buy them in whatever form I might find them and, with the help of a little expert hand, they can become anything from unique tablecloths to placemats or napkins.

Department stores in distant lands are often sources of inspiration (especially if it's the sales period!). Flea markets are obviously a favorite place to discover plates, glasses, and tablecloths of any kind. I tend to buy things without knowing in advance where or how they will be used: schemes and combinations can be made up later, when the pieces have joined the linen closet. (The ideal would be to have a kind of "dressing room" for kitchenware and table linens, to have everything before your eyes every time you need to make a choice... though I grant you that would take up some space.)

As the seasons and years pass, embellish and add to your collections with colored or patterned plates, exotic fabrics, floral or geometric tablecloths and napkins, etched glasses... If you always keep an eye out for things you like, and don't worry too much about always finding complete sets, you'll find that your collection grows into an assortment of objects that reflect your character and your travels—and nothing is more charming than the variety of taste and experience.

A FEW GUIDELINES TO KEEP IN MIND

I have learned many simple tips from my own experience and from hosts and hostesses that I admire. Some appear scattered throughout the book, like seasoning on my menus; but here are a few more basic rules to entertaining the Parisian way that I would like to share with you.

• Give yourself enough time to prepare your meal and set your table. Practice makes perfect. Do not set the bar too high. Start with one of the easier recipes and try it with your family or close friends. Your guests will appreciate you being happy and relaxed and able to enjoy their company, more than if you are totally exhausted from your efforts.

• Be sure to ask your guests ahead of time if they have any food allergies or intolerances. This may be a sign of the times, but can avoid having a guest or a couple say, "Oh, we're allergic to..."—which will dash your enthusiasm for the meal you've just prepared.

• Buy the best ingredients your budget will allow. A simple meal with good, fresh, and, whenever possible, organic ingredients will be appreciated more than a meal that has too many ingredients and risks having no life to it.

• If a guest asks, "What can I bring?"—be specific! Tell your guest what type or brand of red or white wine to bring, or which bottle of champagne, or even exactly which tart from which patisserie for dessert. Not only will they be contributing to the dinner, but you may be helping them discover something new that they can serve again one day themselves.

• Make sure cold drinks are served cold! Even if champagne is in the refrigerator, I like to move it to the freezer an hour before I serve it. For white wine and beer in the refrigerator, move to the freezer 30 minutes before serving. And always be sure you have at least a bag or a couple of trays of ice cubes in the freezer, especially in the summer!

• Slice bread at the last minute before putting it on the table to make sure it stays fresh.

• Do not put a plastic bottle of mineral water on the table. An inexpensive clear glass pitcher will add to making your family and guests feel special.

• Do not overdo pre-dinner cocktails or hors d'œuvres. One hour is the maximum! And keep your hors d'œuvres light—otherwise you risk letting your guests become too full or too tipsy before dinner.

• Make friends with your butcher, baker, fishmonger, and grocer wherever you can. There will be times when you might need to call on them for a favor or a last-minute SOS!

• Check to be sure glasses, plates, and silverware are spot-free so you are not stuck washing or rinsing just before guests arrive. And delegate when you can!

• Check your oven regularly to make sure it is clean to avoid any smoky incidents. It usually happens that the one time you do not check it is the time it starts to smoke from leftover grease.

• One of my best friends—Dodie Rosenkrans, who was a renowned hostess—taught me long ago: "If you accept an invitation, you have an obligation to be a good guest!" Words to live by!

PANTRY AND REFRIGERATOR SUGGESTIONS

Be sure to do a weekly check on your pantry / refrigerator basics and check the expiration date on the package. Depending on your tastes, here are my suggestions for a well stocked pantry / refrigerator:

• A good quality olive oil, butter, milk, fresh eggs

• At least two kinds of pasta: I like to keep spaghetti and penne (gluten-free for certain regular guests)

• A piece of good parmesan cheese

• Dry beans and legumes: lentils, pinto beans, white beans, chick peas

• Grains: couscous, bulgur, quinoa, polenta

• Nuts: pine nuts, pistachios, whole almonds

• Rice: risotto and brown rice, white rice

• Condiments: Dijon mustard, whole grain mustard, ketchup

• Vinegars: red wine, white wine, sherry, aged balsamic

• Soy sauce

• Packets of dry or cartons of organic stock: fish, chicken, vegetable

• A jar of good anchovies in olive oil

• 2 cans of good quality Italian tomatoes and passata

• Capers in salt

• Red chile pepper flakes, black peppercorns for the peppermill, Maldon or a good sea salt

• Dry herbs and spices: cumin seeds, fennel seeds, nutmeg, oregano

• Fresh herbs: Italian parsley, cilantro, basil

• 2 or 3 fresh organic lemons

WEEKDAY MENUS

BAKED SEA BASS
BROCCOLI, AVOCADO, FENNEL, AND CILANTRO SALAD

This is a great recipe for those Mondays that follow a weekend of over-indulgence. Fish bought from the market on Sunday, served with an assortment of vegetables, will compensate for all those calories you consumed!

TO SERVE 4

FOR THE SEA BASS

4 medium size fresh sea bass, gutted and scaled (1 per person)

Herb-flavored salt

Trimmings of a fennel bulb (the bulb will be used in the salad)

1 tablespoon olive oil

Ask your fish seller to gut and scale the sea bass.

Preheat the oven to 400°F (210°C). Line a rimmed baking dish (a baking sheet) that's large enough to hold all the fish with baking paper or foil. Season the insides of the fish generously with the salt and place the fennel trimmings in each cavity.

Place a few sticks of fennel on the baking dish and lay the fish side by side on top of the fennel sticks—this will help you remove the fish from the baking pan and ensure that they cook through. Drizzle with the olive oil and cook for 20 minutes. Use a paring knife to test if fish is done by piercing and checking to be sure the flesh is white and not translucent.

FOR THE SALAD

1 large head broccoli	1 bunch cilantro
Salt	Juice of 1 lemon
1 fennel bulb	3 tablespoons olive oil
1 large, ripe avocado	Freshly ground black pepper

Wash the broccoli and cut it into florets. Bring a pot of salted water to a boil and briefly blanch the florets for 3 minutes; they should remain crunchy. Drain and allow to cool.

Slice the fennel bulb and pit, dice, and peel the avocado. Wash and chop the cilantro. Combine all the ingredients in a salad bowl.

To prepare the dressing, whisk together the lemon juice, olive oil, salt, and pepper to taste to form an emulsion. Pour it over the salad just before serving.

VEAL BURGERS
WARM SMOKY SAUTÉED MUSHROOMS
FRESH HERB SALAD

This is a real guest pleaser, so easy and yet so good! The juicy veal burger flavored with mixed fresh herbs paired with the sautéed mushrooms with smoky paprika is an out-of-this-world combination. You can easily adapt this menu to serve eight people. Serve it with ice cold beer or a nice chilled red.

TO SERVE 4

FOR THE VEAL BURGERS AND HERB SALAD

1 bunch tarragon	1¾ pounds (800 g) ground veal
1 bunch chervil	Salt and freshly ground black pepper
1 bunch flat-leaf parsley	Olive oil
½ bunch chives	Sherry vinegar

Wash and dry the herbs. Roughly chop up a few sprigs of each of the herbs and chives. Gently mix the herbs into the ground veal. Season with salt and pepper.

Using your hands, make 4 thick patties from the veal mixture. Set aside until ready to cook.

When the herb salad and mushrooms are ready, heat a little olive oil in a skillet over high heat and briefly sear the patties on each side. Reduce the heat to low and cook them for an additional 10 minutes, turning the patties over after 5 minutes.

FOR THE HERB SALAD

Pick the leaves off the remaining herbs, snip chives into bite-size pieces with kitchen scissors, and put in a salad bowl. Dress with the vinegar and olive oil. Toss gently. Salt and pepper to taste.

Serve the salad alongside the veal burgers and mushrooms.

FOR THE SMOKY SAUTÉED MUSHROOMS

1 ¼ pounds (600 g) mushrooms

Olive oil

Salt

2 garlic cloves, finely chopped

2 tablespoons pimentón or other smoked paprika

About 4 tablespoons chopped flat-leaf parsley

Wash the mushrooms under cold running water. Dry them well, slightly trim bottom of stem, and cut them into quarters. Heat the olive oil in a skillet and sauté the mushrooms. Season them with salt so that the mushrooms render all of their water; pour some off if there is too much liquid. Add the garlic and pimentón. Drizzle in a little more olive oil and cook for a few minutes further, stirring, until the garlic is nicely golden. Scatter with the parsley.

HELPFUL HINT: *Buy the best ingredients your budget will allow. A simple meal with good, fresh, and, whenever possible, organic ingredients will be appreciated more than a meal that has too many ingredients and risks having no life to it.*

MARINATED CHICKEN
CAESAR SALAD
STRAWBERRY AND PISTACHIO ICE CREAM

This combination of juicy, pan-seared chicken breasts with a light, lemony take on the classic Caesar salad will likely become one of your go-to menus, for both weekday meals and casual summer entertaining. Chicken breasts can be dry and tasteless, but if you take the time to marinate and avoid overcooking them, you'll achieve juicy results. Marinate the chicken while you make the Caesar salad.

TO SERVE 4

FOR THE SALAD

2 small heads romaine lettuce or
6 small heads gem lettuce

6 medium-sized mushrooms

1 ripe medium-sized avocado

½ cup of shaved parmesan shavings

FOR THE SALAD DRESSING

½ garlic clove, sliced

Juice of 1 medium size lemon

5 anchovy filets (packed in olive oil)

½ cup (50 g) grated Parmigiano

5 tablespoons (75 ml) olive oil

Salt and freshly ground black pepper

Wash and dry the lettuces. If using gem, separate the leaves before washing. If using romaine, tear the washed and dried leaves into bite-size pieces by hand, leaving the smaller leaves whole.

Wash the mushrooms, trim the very bottom of the stem, and dry them using paper towels, then slice them. Peel and pit the avocado and cut the flesh into thick slices. Place the vegetables in a salad bowl, making sure to place the mushrooms over the lettuce and the avocado on the mushrooms.

To make the dressing, in a mixing glass deep enough to use an immersion blender, first combine the garlic, lemon juice, and anchovies. Gradually add grated Parmigiano, 2 pinches of salt, and drizzle in the olive oil. Blend to make a fairly thick dressing. Adjust the salt and season with pepper, adding a little more olive oil if necessary.

Using a Y-shaped vegetable peeler, shave curls of Parmigiano off a piece of cheese. Pour the salad dressing over the salad, toss to combine, and scatter with the Parmigiano shavings.

FOR THE CHICKEN

1 garlic clove, chopped

Juice of ½ lemon

2 pinches peperoncino

2 tablespoons olive oil

**2 chicken breasts,
boned and cut in half but not flattened**

Whisk together the garlic, lemon juice, chili powder, and olive oil in a large bowl, add the chicken breasts, and allow to marinate for 30 minutes at room temperature.

Set a large skillet over high heat, remove the chicken breast from the marinade, and cook until nicely browned on both sides. Test for doneness by slicing into the breast after cooking for 15 minutes. Cut into slices against the grain, and serve alongside the Caesar salad.

FOR THE DESSERT

Use an ice cream scoop to make a single scoop that combines the strawberry and pistachio ice creams; this is done by making a half-scoop of each flavor in one scoop. Sprinkle with chopped fresh pistachios. Make remaining servings. This dessert is easy, great looking, and so good!

LINGUINE WITH GENOVESE PESTO

_____

This is an easy pasta dish that is quite a surprise because of the potatoes and green beans,
which pair perfectly together with the pesto.
I like to start with a couple of different salads, such as a mixed green salad and a buratta with fava beans.

TO SERVE 6

FOR THE LINGUINE

Leaves of 1 bunch basil, washed and dried

1 clove garlic, chopped

⅔ cup (150 ml) extra-virgin olive oil

Salt

3½ ounces (100 g) Parmigiano or pecorino, freshly grated (about ½ cup), plus freshly grated Parmigiano to serve

2 ounces (50 g) pine nuts or pistachios (about ⅓ cup)

1 pound (450 g) dry linguine

4 medium size potatoes, about 1 lb

5 ounces (150 g) extra fine green beans, haricots verts, trimmed

First make the pesto: Working in brief pulses, process the basil leaves with the garlic, oil, and a pinch of salt. Add the grated Parmigiano and the pine nuts and process until smooth.

Cook the potatoes in boiling salted water, then drain and dice them. Choose the dish or bowl that you will serve from and set them aside.

Cook the pasta in boiling salted water according to directions on the package, together with the green beans. Drain, setting aside about 1 cup of the cooking water. Pour some of the hot cooking water into the serving dish to heat it up. Add the pesto and potatoes to the pan with the pasta and beans, pouring in a little of the saved pasta cooking water if necessary to thin the sauce. Toss gently. Discard the water in the serving dish and transfer the pasta pesto mixture to the dish.

Serve with freshly grated Parmigiano.

Since the pesto keeps very well for a few days when refrigerated, go ahead and increase the quantities so you can enjoy it later with grilled vegetables or a tomato and mozzarella salad.

OVEN-ROASTED SALMON
POTATO SALAD
RAW AND COOKED BEET SALAD
CUCUMBERS WITH YOGURT

———————————

This meal is sure to renew your appreciation of salmon. The distinct tastes and textures of the two salads and the tangy cucumbers with yogurt perfectly complement the salmon—and each other. I serve this menu as a light dinner or for Sunday brunch, when I swap the cooked salmon for smoked salmon.

Take advantage of the different colors of each dish to set an interesting table. I used a bright pink washable-paper place setting with a mix of different colored plates, bowls, and dishes. Bright blue linen napkins and red water glasses serve as accents.

TO SERVE 6

FOR THE POTATO SALAD

1 ¾ pounds (800 g) baby potatoes, unpeeled

1 small spring onion

10 gherkins

1 tablespoon capers packed in salt

A few sprigs flat-leaf parsley

¼ cup (60 ml) olive oil

2 tablespoons sherry vinegar

2 tablespoons Dijon mustard

Salt and freshly ground black pepper

Cook the potatoes in salted boiling water for about 20 minutes. Check for doneness with the tip of a knife; the knife should slide in easily. Rinse the potatoes under cold running water and cut them into halves, retaining the skin. Peel and slice the onion. Cut the gherkins into rounds. Wash the salt off the capers. Combine all the ingredients in a mixing bowl. To make the dressing, whisk together the olive oil, vinegar, mustard, and salt and pepper to taste. Transfer the salad to a serving dish and carefully toss with the dressing. Serve warm or chilled—it's equally delicious either way.

FOR THE BEET SALAD

2 small raw beets

2 cooked medium size beets

2 tablespoons balsamic vinegar

¼ cup (60 ml) olive oil

Fleur de sel and freshly ground pepper

A few sprigs dill

Peel the cooked and raw beets. Using a mandoline, slice the raw beets, quartering them if necessary. Cut the cooked beets into a large dice. Place in a serving bowl. Combine the vinegar and oil to make the dressing and stir it into the beets. Scatter with sprigs of dill. Serve at room temperature.

FOR THE CUCUMBERS WITH YOGURT

2 Persian cucumbers or
1 medium size cucumber

10 ounces (300 g) Greek yogurt

½ clove garlic, crushed

3 tablespoons olive oil

Juice of 1 lemon

1 tablespoon white wine vinegar

Salt and freshly ground black pepper

A few sprigs dill, chopped

Peel the cucumbers and slice them in half lengthwise. With a teaspoon, scoop out the seeds. Cut the lengths into evenly shaped half-moons.

Pour the yogurt into a salad bowl. Stir in the crushed garlic, olive oil, lemon juice, and vinegar. Season with salt and pepper and mix well. Stir the cucumber and dill into the mixture.

FOR THE SALMON

6 salmon fillets with skin

Olive oil as needed

Preheat the oven to 400°F (210°C). Oil a baking sheet and arrange the salmon fillets on it skin side down. Lightly brush each fillet with more oil. Place on the middle oven rack and bake for about 15 – 20 minutes. (This cooking time is for fillets that are approximately 1 inch [2.5 to 3 cm] thick, so you may need to adjust slightly.)

ROAST RACK OF LAMB WITH PAN JUICES
GREEN TABBOULEH

———————————

This is another meal that can easily be expanded to accommodate the number of guests—and the size of the rack of lamb. The tabbouleh is a healthy, delicious accompaniment for the lamb, and the sumac gives it just the right touch of the exotic. A lemon or pear sorbet would be the perfect dessert.

TO SERVE 4

FOR THE LAMB

1 rack of lamb with 8 chops

3 tablespoons olive oil

2 cloves garlic, crushed

Salt and freshly ground black pepper

Preheat the oven to 450°F (240°C). To prepare the rack of lamb, brush it with oil and season with salt and pepper. Place in a roasting dish or roasting pan and roast for 10 minutes, then reduce the temperature to 400°F (210°C) and turn the rack over. Roast for an additional 15 minutes. Remove lamb from the oven (leaving the oven on), place on a cutting board, and tent with a sheet of foil. Deglaze the pan juices with ¾ cup (200 ml) water, incorporating the crushed garlic. Return the roasting dish to the oven and allow the liquid to reduce by half. You can also put the roasting pan over a medium-low heat to reduce more quickly. Strain through a fine-mesh sieve into a bowl, transfer the rack of lamb to a warm serving platter, and pour the pan juices over the top.

FOR THE TABBOULEH

1 small glass medium-grain whole bulgur

2 bunches flat-leaf parsley

1 bunch mint

2 spring onions, with greens

2 lemons

1 teaspoon sumac

Salt and freshly ground black pepper

Scant ⅓ cup (75 ml) olive oil

Place the bulgur in a bowl of boiling water for 15 minutes to soften. Wash the parsley, pick off the leaves, and chop them finely. Wash the mint and pick off the leaves; cut them to a width of just under ½ inch (1 cm). Slice the scallions very finely and combine them with the herbs in a salad bowl. When the bulgur no longer has any crunch, remove it from the water and drain using a fine-mesh strainer. Combine it with the other ingredients in the salad bowl. Squeeze the two lemons and stir the juice into the salad. Add the salt, pepper, and olive oil and toss to combine.

Serve this salad with baba ganoush and/or hummus. Heat pita bread in the oven until crisp to serve on the side.

SKATE WITH CAPER–LEMON ZEST GREMOLATA
THREE-TOMATO SALAD

A delicious—and super light!—summer dinner that pairs poached fish with a caper–lemon zest gremolata and a colorful tomato salad. Take advantage of the different varieties of tomatoes that are available during the season.

Use brightly colored table accents to keep the summer theme going. You don't have to spend a lot of money: I used washable recycled-fabric place settings and cloth napkins I bought on sale, plus some inexpensive bamboo and lacquer bowls.

TO SERVE 4

FOR THE SALAD

6 organic ripe tomatoes, in different sizes and colors

Salt

Olive oil

Freshly ground black pepper

A few small basil leaves

Using a paring knife, peel the tomatoes and slice them thinly, about ¼ inch (5 mm) thick. Arrange the slices on a platter and sprinkle with a little salt so that they will render some of their liquid. Allow them to rest for 30 minutes, then remove as much of the juice as possible by tipping the platter. Drizzle the tomatoes with a little olive oil, adjust the salt and season with pepper, and garnish with the basil leaves.

Note: You don't have to peel the tomatoes, but once you've tried them prepared like this, you'll be a convert! The skin of organic, ripe tomatoes should peel easily. If they don't, I suggest just slicing them so they look great in the salad.

FOR THE SKATE

A few sprigs flat-leaf parsley

Capers packed in salt

Grated zest of 1 lemon

Olive oil

Salt and freshly ground black pepper

2 tablespoons packaged court-bouillon mix (contains coarse salt, spices, and assorted herbs); otherwise, Old Bay Seasoning may be used

1 skate wing (about 1¾ pounds / 800 g), cut into four portions

Wash the parsley, pick off the leaves, and chop them. Rinse the capers in hot water to remove the salt, and then chop them. With a zester remove the lemon peel and chop it finely. Combine the parsley, capers, and lemon zest with enough olive oil to make a fairly thick green sauce. Season with salt and pepper.

Flavor a pot of water with the court-bouillon mix and bring it to a boil. Place the pieces of fish in the water. Once it returns to a boil, remove the pot from the heat, put the lid on the pot, and allow the fish to poach in the hot water for about 10 minutes.

With a slotted spoon, carefully remove the pieces of skate. Allow them to cool, then carefully remove the flesh from the cartilage and serve, accompanied by the gremolata.

FUSILLI WITH SAUSAGE

———————

This is one of the best, easiest, and most satisfying meals you will ever make. My grandmother made a version of this, which I have always remembered, and Sicilian friends helped me rediscover this as well. It's another "comfort" dinner that you will make often for family and friends. Serve with a simple broccoli salad dressed with a fresh lemon juice vinaigrette. Fresh strawberries drizzled with aged balsamic vinegar make a light, delicious dessert!

TO SERVE 4

2 heaping teaspoons fennel seeds

Olive oil

3 Toulouse sausages or other good-quality pork sausages

1 teaspoon crushed red pepper flakes, ideally pepperoncino

1 small glass dry white wine

1 teaspoon dried oregano

Grated zest and juice of 1 lemon

1 pound (450 g) good-quality fusilli

2 tablespoons butter

4 oz. grated Parmigiano

A few sprigs flat-leaf parsley leaves, chopped

Salt and freshly ground black pepper

Crush the fennel seeds using a mortar and pestle. Heat a drizzle of olive oil in a large skillet. Remove the sausage filling from the casings and place it in the skillet. Cook over medium high heat, stirring constantly, for a few minutes, until the meat has colored. Crumble it with a fork so that you don't have any large pieces. Add the fennel and crushed red pepper and continue cooking until the meat is well browned. Deglaze with the white wine and allow the liquid to reduce by half. Stir in the oregano and the lemon zest and juice. Reduce the heat to low while you cook the pasta, so the mixture stays warm.

In a large pot of salted boiling water, cook the pasta according to the directions on the package. Drain in a colander, reserving some of the cooking liquid.

Combine the pasta with the meat in the skillet and stir in the butter, Parmigiano, and parsley. To ensure that your sauce is lovely and shiny, stir in 2 tablespoons of the pasta cooking liquid. Salt and pepper to taste. Serve, topped with a sprinkling of grated Parmigiano.

COD WITH CILANTRO PESTO
WATERCRESS SALAD WITH MUSHROOMS, CUCUMBERS, AND AVOCADO
BERRY TRIFLE

This is an easy, delicious, healthy dinner for weekdays or weekends. The watercress salad, with buttery avocado and a Dijon dressing, will likely become a favorite, prepared to accompany roasted chicken, grilled steaks, or other grilled or baked fish dishes. I enjoy finishing the meal with this berry trifle, a simple dessert that looks more sinful than it actually is!

TO SERVE 4

FOR THE SALAD

1 bunch watercress

2 Persian cucumbers

1 bunch cilantro

6 medium-sized mushrooms

1 ripe medium-sized avocado

2 tablespoons old-fashioned (grainy) Dijon mustard

Juice of ½ lemon

⅓ cup (75 ml) olive oil

Salt and freshly ground black pepper

Wash and drain the watercress and remove any thick stalks. Peel the cucumbers, cut them in half lengthwise, and scoop the seeds out with a teaspoon. Cut the cucumbers into half-moons that are fairly thick. Wash the cilantro and chop it roughly. Wash the mushrooms under cold running water, trim the bottom of the stems, pat them dry using paper towels, and slice them. Halve the avocado, remove the pit, and dice the flesh. Combine all the ingredients in a large salad bowl. To prepare the dressing, mix together the mustard, lemon juice, olive oil, salt, and pepper to form an emulsion. Pour it over the salad at the last moment and toss gently just before serving.

FOR THE COD

2 tablespoons court-bouillon mix (contains coarse salt, spices, and assorted herbs); Old Bay Seasoning may also be used

1 thick cod fillet (1 to 1½ pounds / 455 to 680 g), cut into 4 portions

1 bunch cilantro

½ garlic clove

3 tablespoons olive oil

Juice of ½ lemon

Salt and freshly ground black pepper

In a large pot, bring water flavored with the court-bouillon mix to a boil. Gently place the fish portions in the pot and cover with the lid. When the water returns to a boil, remove the pot from the heat and let the fish poach. Your fish needs only 10 minutes to be perfectly cooked; it will remain slightly translucent.

While the fish is cooking, combine the cilantro with the garlic, olive oil, lemon juice, salt, and pepper to taste and puree to make a green coulis—your cilantro pesto.

Spread the pesto over the bottom of a serving dish. Carefully remove the fish from the court-bouillon using a slotted spoon and place it on the bed of pesto. Serve with new potatoes that require no more than simple boiling.

FOR THE BERRY TRIFLE

Store-bought meringues

1 package fresh red currants, strawberries, or other berries of your choice

Whipped cream

Store-bought red berry coulis or purée

With your hands, crumble the meringues into large pieces. Reserve some of the berries for the garnish. Arrange some meringue crumbles as the base in four dessert bowls, then divide the coulis and berries among the bowls, alternating with additional crumbled meringue to create layers. Finish with a lovely dollop of whipped cream and decorate with the few remaining berries.

WATERCRESS SOUP
FRENCH MAC 'N' CHEESE

This is true comfort food with a French "accent": simple, good home cooking! If you've never had watercress soup, you're in for a treat: Warm, soothing, and delicious, there is just something about a bowl of homemade watercress soup that always makes you feel better. Follow the soup with my mac and cheese—it is an airier version of what you have known up until now with a delightfully crunchy crust. Served with a glass of good red wine, this is winter comfort food at its best.

TO SERVE 4

FOR THE SOUP

2 packets powdered chicken bouillon

4 cups (1 L) boiling water

Note: You may also substitute 4 cups of organic chicken broth for the above 2 ingredients

2 bunches watercress

2 medium-sized potatoes

2 tablespoons butter

1 yellow onion, chopped

A few walnuts optional

Soak the packets of chicken stock in the boiling water.

Trim the stalks of each bunch of watercress, cutting them so you have about 2 inches of stem. Wash and clean well, and drain. Peel the potatoes and cut them into cubes.

In a large pot, heat the butter. When it begins to sizzle, add the onion and sweat it. Add the watercress and potatoes to the pot. When the watercress has wilted, pour in the chicken stock. The liquid level should be at least two fingers higher than the vegetables. Cook until the potatoes are completely softened, and then blitz the soup with an immersion blender until creamy.

Serve while still nice and hot, scattered with a few walnuts.

FOR THE MAC 'N' CHEESE

8 ounces (250 g) Comté or artisanal cheddar cheese, grated, plus a little more for the topping

200 ml whipping cream

¼ nutmeg nut

14 ounces (400 g) rigatoni (or use the largest tube pasta you can find)

2 tablespoons butter

2 slices melba toast

Mixed salad greens, such as mesclun

Salt and freshly ground black pepper

Set the oven to broil and preheat. Butter an ovenproof dish.

Cook the rigatoni following the directions on the package.

While pasta is cooking: In a large skillet over very low heat, melt the cheese, making sure to stir with a wooden spoon and gradually stir in the cream until the mixture is smooth. Grate the nutmeg over the melted cheese and cream. Add salt and pepper to taste.

Drain the pasta and transfer to a buttered ovenproof dish. Using a wooden spoon, spread the melted sauce over the rigatoni and gently mix until all of the pasta has been mixed evenly with the sauce. Crush the melba toast with your hands to make crumbs and sprinkle them over the top of the dish, then add a little extra grated cheese and dot with butter. Bake under the broiler for about 10 minutes, until the topping is crisp and brown.

Serve the mac 'n' cheese with a salad of mixed greens.

RISOTTO PRIMAVERA
FRENCH BEAN SALAD

Risotto primavera is the perfect way to welcome spring and celebrate the first signs that winter is behind us—in this case with fresh fava beans and garden peas.
Do not be intimidated by the prospect of making risotto. Practice makes perfect, and you will feel accomplished once you've mastered this favorite and added it to your list of go-to dishes! When risotto is on the menu, I always try to keep the starter simple, and this green bean and feta salad is sure to please.

I chose a daisy theme for the table, using an embroidered tablecloth and napkins I found at the neighborhood brocante, or flea market, mixed with Japanese enamel bowls I ordered online and some Murano glasses with a similar motif.

TO SERVE 4

FOR THE RISOTTO

4 cups (1 liter) chicken or vegetable stock

8 spears green asparagus

14 ounces (400 g) fresh fava beans

14 ounces (400 g) fresh garden peas

Salt

2 tablespoons olive oil

1 onion, finely chopped

2 stalks celery, trimmed and finely chopped

14 ounces (400 g) Arborio rice

1 small glass dry white wine

Freshly ground pepper

5 tablespoons (70 g) butter

3½ ounces (100 g) Parmigiano, freshly grated

Heat the stock in a saucepan. Trim and discard the bases of the asparagus stalks. Set aside the tips and slice the stalks crosswise into small ½ inch pieces. Cook the fava beans and shelled peas for 5 minutes in a pot of boiling salted water. Using a large slotted spoon, remove the beans and peas from the boiling water. Drain and remove the white skin from the fava beans. In the same water used to cook the favas and peas, blanch the asparagus pieces until just al dente, for about 5 minutes.

Heat the olive oil in a deep, heavy bottomed sauté pan and gently cook the onion and celery for 15 minutes. Stir in the rice and increase the heat to a low medium; it should become translucent after 1 minute. Pour in the white wine, stirring constantly (the alcohol will evaporate). When the rice has absorbed the wine, pour in a ladleful of hot stock.

Reduce the heat to low and continue cooking, stirring constantly. Gradually add ladlefuls of the stock over the course of 20 minutes, then taste the rice to check for doneness—it should be tender.

Add the fava beans, peas, and asparagus stalks to the pan, reserving the asparagus tips for decoration. Season with salt and pepper. Remove the pan from the heat and stir in the butter and Parmigiano. Mix well, cover with the lid, and allow to rest for 2 minutes. Serve immediately, garnished with the asparagus tips.

If you prefer, you can stop the cooking process just before the vegetables are added. Then, when it's almost time to serve, gently reheat the rice, add the vegetables, and finish as described above.

FOR THE FRENCH BEANS

1 ¾ pounds (800 g) French beans, or fine green beans

7 ounces (200 g) feta cheese

Grated lemon zest

3 tablespoons olive oil

Balsamic vinegar to drizzle over green beans

Salt and freshly ground black pepper

Wash and trim the beans. Cook them in a pot of salted boiling water for about 10 minutes, until al dente. Drain them and dunk them in a bowl of very cold water so that they retain their greenness. Place drained beans on paper towels to dry. Arrange the beans on individual serving plates and scatter with crumbly feta cheese and a little lemon zest. Drizzle with the olive oil and balsamic vinegar and add a few turns of freshly ground black pepper.

FOR THE DESSERT

Ask your guests to bring a dessert such as a lemon tart to serve as a final flourish to this spring lunch.

MONKFISH STEW
GRATED CARROTS AND ZUCCHINI SALAD
WARM QUINOA SALAD

I have had many versions of this soup in many countries, but I find this to be my favorite and the easiest version to make. Monkfish steaks are what I prefer to use, but you can use any solid white fish that will stay together when it is cooked in the tomato sauce. I serve a warm quinoa salad with this, which soaks up the tasty tomato sauce. You can prepare the sauce ahead of time and then heat it up and add it to the fish to cook. This allows you to spend some time with your guests before dinner.

TO SERVE 6

FOR THE GRATED CARROTS AND ZUCCHINI

2 carrots

2 yellow zucchini

2 green zucchini

2 tablespoons sesame seeds

¼ cup (60 ml) olive oil

Juice of 1 lemon

Salt and freshly ground black pepper

Wash, peel, and grate the carrots. Wash and grate the zucchini.

In a skillet, toast the sesame seeds until they are golden.

To make the dressing, whisk together the olive oil, lemon juice, salt, and pepper. Drizzle the dressing over the grated vegetables and gently toss. Test for salt and pepper. Just before serving, sprinkle with the toasted sesame seeds. And of course, should you be so inspired, feel free to add freshly chopped cilantro and a pinch of crushed ground chili pepper!

FOR THE MONKFISH STEW

2¼ pounds (1 kg) monkfish steaks, about 1 inch (2.5 cm) thick, rinsed and patted dry with paper towels

1 medium-sized yellow onion, diced

2 medium-sized cloves garlic, root removed, finely chopped

3 stalks celery, peeled and chopped

Leaves of ¾ bunch flat-leaf parsley, washed, dried, and roughly chopped

4 tablespoons olive oil

1 cup white wine

2 16-oz cans Italian cherry tomatoes or whole plum tomatoes, crushed by hand, with the juice

¼ teaspoon crushed red pepper flakes

½ teaspoon salt

Zest of 1 organic lemon, finely chopped

Juice of ½ an organic lemon

In a heavy pan, preferably large enough to hold the fish steaks in one layer, heat the olive oil over medium heat and add the onion. Stir using a wooden spoon and cook for 4 to 5 minutes until the onion becomes translucent. Add the garlic and cook for 4 to 5 minutes longer, making sure not to brown the onion or the garlic. Add the chopped celery and cook for another 4 to 5 minutes. Add the chopped parsley and stir to combine. Cook for about 2 minutes and pour in the white wine. After the wine has cooked with the vegetables for about 3 minutes, add the tomatoes with their juice and let the sauce cook on a low bubbling simmer for about 20 minutes, until the sauce has slightly thickened.

Stir in the red pepper flakes and taste for salt, adjusting as needed. Add the fish steaks, cover the pot, and cook them for 8 to 10 minutes on each side. Note: A less dense fish will cook in less time, so check for doneness early!

Five minutes before the fish is finished cooking, add the lemon zest and juice, and gently stir it into the stew, so you do not break up the fish.

As this is a simple dish, I like serving it in the pan that it is cooked in, but you can transfer it to a heated serving bowl or deep platter if you prefer.

FOR THE WARM QUINOA SALAD

1 ½ cups (300 g) quinoa

¼ cup whole almonds, slightly crushed in a mortar

¼ cup whole sunflower seeds, shelled

¼ cup whole cashews, slightly crushed in a mortar

Salt and freshly ground black pepper

⅓ bunch of washed and dried Italian parsley leaves, roughly chopped

⅓ bunch of washed and dried cilantro leaves, roughly chopped

½ cup chopped green onions

Cook the quinoa according to the package instructions, but do not overcook it as it will continue to cook while draining. Make sure not to salt the quinoa until it is done.

Toast the almonds, sunflower seeds, and cashews in the oven at 320°F (160°C) until they begin to brown. Salt and pepper the toasted nuts and seeds. (Celery salt is great for this.)

Put the quinoa into a serving bowl and add the salted seeds and nuts, the parsley, cilantro, and green onions. Toss and add salt and pepper accordingly. Serve alongside the fish soup.

PUMPKIN SOUP
ROAST VEAL
HERBY MASHED POTATOES

———————

This comforting meal will remind you of going to your aunt and uncle's house for Sunday dinner. It is fairly easy to prepare, yet your guests or family will feel like they are getting the royal treatment, especially if you finish with a dessert. Even a very easy one, like the scoops of chocolate sorbet topped with candied orange peel that I suggest, keeps the meal feeling special. Make sure you serve your soup piping hot and that your potatoes are smooth and warm.

I have used my grandmother's dishes, mixed with a collection of family silver, to make the table setting more traditional.

TO SERVE 6

FOR THE ROAST VEAL

One 3-pound (1.5 kg) veal roast

Salt and freshly ground black pepper

4 shallots, unpeeled and halved

1 bunch fresh thyme

Olive oil

Scant ½ cup (100 ml) dry hard apple cider

Preheat the oven to 375°F (190°C).

Season the veal with salt and pepper. Place it in an ovenproof dish and arrange the cut shallots and thyme around it. Drizzle with a little olive oil. Roast for about 20 to 25 minutes, the meat should have begun to brown. Pour the hard cider into the dish and return it to the oven for an additional 15 minutes. Just before the cooking time is up, baste the meat and shallots with the cooking juices. Slice the roast and serve with the herby mashed potatoes, the softened shallots, and the delicious cooking juices.

FOR THE SOUP

2 pumpkin quarters

1 yellow onion

2 Tablespoons butter

Salt and freshly ground black pepper

Juice of ½ orange

Pumpkin seeds

Peel the pumpkin and cut the flesh into large cubes. Slice the onion. Melt the butter in a large pot and sweat the onion. Add the pumpkin to the pot and sauté the cubes for a few minutes; do not allow them to color brown. Pour in just enough water to cover the pumpkin and no more. Allow to simmer gently for 30 minutes.

Season with salt and pepper and pour in the orange juice. Blend using an immersion blender. Adjust the seasoning if necessary. Just before serving, scatter pumpkin seeds over the soup.

FOR THE HERBY MASHED POTATOES

2¼ pounds (1 kg) potatoes, for mashing

Salt

2 garlic cloves, peeled

1 bunch parsley

5 tablespoons (75 g) butter

1 small glass milk

Freshly ground black pepper

Wash, peel, and halve the potatoes. Cook them for about 20 minutes in a large pot of boiling salted water with the garlic cloves. Check for doneness with the tip of a knife. Wash the parsley, pick off the leaves, and chop them. Drain the potatoes and return them to the pot with the boiled garlic cloves, butter, and milk. Mash with a potato ricer. Season with salt and pepper and stir in the chopped parsley. Cover the pot with the lid and keep warm over very low heat.

FOR THE DESSERT

A scoop of chocolate sorbet, served in an attractive glass and topped with candied orange peel, is the perfect finale to this simple fall dinner.

GEM LETTUCE WITH ANCHOVIES
LINGUINE WITH PRAWNS AND ARUGULA

Fresh prawns, peppery arugula, and cherry tomatoes tossed with pasta make for a colorful, satisfying main course that is easy and casual. Call your fish vendor ahead of time as the freshness of the prawns is key. A pinch of red pepper flakes and lemon zest add the necessary oomph.

Serve with hearts of romaine topped with good-quality anchovy fillets, a drizzle of olive oil, and a sprinkle of Piment d'Espelette, and you'll have a meal that will dazzle your family or friends.

TO SERVE 4

FOR THE SALAD

8 heads gem lettuce

16 anchovy fillets packed in oil

Maldon salt

Crushed Piment d'Espelette (a mild chili pepper from the Basque region) or other mild chili pepper

Olive oil for drizzling

Rinse the heads of lettuce under running water. Drain them, dry them, trim the bases. Cut them in two lengthwise and place an anchovy fillet on each half. Sprinkle with a little Maldon salt and piment d'Espelette to taste and drizzle with olive oil.

Note: Salad may be prepared first and dressed at the last minute.

FOR THE PASTA

1 pound (450 g) linguine

Olive oil

1 garlic clove, peeled and chopped

2 pinches crushed red pepper, ideally peperoncino

Zest and juice of ½ lemon

About 15 cherry tomatoes, halved

1 small glass white wine

14 ounces (400 g) raw shelled prawns / jumbo shrimp

Salt

2 handfuls arugula, roughly chopped

Cook the pasta in a large pot of boiling salted water according to package directions. Meanwhile, in a large skillet, warm the olive oil. Over a medium high heat, add the garlic, red pepper flakes, and lemon zest. As soon as the garlic begins to color, add the cherry tomato halves and sauté for 5 minutes. Pour in the white wine and simmer for 5 minutes so the alcohol evaporates. Lastly, add the raw prawns and season with salt. Cook for about 5 more minutes, until just done.

When the pasta is cooked, drain in a colander, reserving the cooking liquid to heat the serving dish and to add to the sauce if necessary. Combine the pasta with the sauce in the pot pasta was cooked in and squeeze in the lemon juice. Stir in two-thirds of the chopped arugula. If the sauce needs a little diluting, incorporate 3 tablespoons of the pasta cooking liquid. Transfer to the serving dish (having discarded cooking water from dish). Divide the pasta among four heated pasta bowls and scatter the remaining arugula leaves over the top of each one.

Helpful Hint: If you cannot find fresh prawns, precooked prawns from your fish vendor can be used. Just be sure you add them to the simmering cherry tomatoes at the last minute, reheating them just until they are hot. Do not overcook precooked prawns!

CAPONATA
SOFT-BOILED EGGS

A Sicilian classic, caponata is a staple in every household as it includes all of the vegetables that are available year-round in Sicily. I like this version as they all go in the oven at the same time and cook together. What could be easier? Once you have tried this, you will be sure to keep a bowl of caponata in your refrigerator!
I have served it here for lunch on toasted country bread topped with a 6-minute boiled egg so the yolk is still slightly soft. The French call this "mollet."

TO SERVE 6

FOR THE CAPONATA

2 large purple eggplant, cut into large chunks

1 green bell pepper, cored and cut into large chunks

1 red bell pepper, cored and cut into large chunks

4 cloves garlic, peeled and cut in half

2 small red onions, quartered

2 green zucchini, cut into rounds

2 yellow zucchini, cut into rounds

Olive oil

8 tomatoes, quartered

2 tablespoons capers packed in salt

1 bunch basil

1 handful raisins

2 tablespoons sherry vinegar

1 handful pine nuts, toasted

Salt and freshly ground black pepper

Preheat the oven to 325°F (160°C).

When all of the vegetables have been washed and cut as indicated, combine the eggplant, bell peppers, garlic, onions, and zucchini in a large ovenproof dish (the tomatoes cook more quickly). Season with salt and pepper and pour over a generous amount of olive oil. Place in the oven to begin baking for 45 minutes. After about 20 minutes, stir the vegetables with a wooden spoon so they are all evenly coated with the oil. After 45 minutes add the tomatoes and increase the oven temperature to 400°F (210°C), which will render the juice of the tomatoes. Cook for an additional 30 minutes. Rinse and drain the capers. Tear a few basil leaves with your hands. Add the capers, the torn basil leaves, as well as the basil stalks to the dish with the raisins and vinegar. Stir well to combine the ingredients and return the dish to the oven for approximately 10 minutes more. Allow to cool to lukewarm, sprinkle with the pine nuts, and serve.

This is an ideal dish for summer that is as good chilled as it is warm. It is the perfect accompaniment to eggs, as well as to grilled fish or meat.

FOR THE EGGS

2 very fresh eggs per person

Bring a pot of water to a boil and carefully place the eggs in it. Once the water returns to a boil, allow 6 minutes for the eggs to cook, then remove them with a slotted spoon and refresh them under cold running water. Gently roll them on your work surface to crack the shell. Working carefully, peel the shells off under a stream of running water. Serve with the caponata and slices of toast.

SMOKED HADDOCK CHOWDER
OPEN-FACED AVOCADO TARTINES

———————

This is one of those meals that you can make for two or ten people without worrying that it won't turn out.
The smoky haddock lends a rich flavor to the vegetables, and the avocado tartines garnished with pomegranate seeds
add a super-fresh touch to a lunch or a casual dinner

TO SERVE 6

FOR THE AVOCADO TARTINES

2 ripe avocados

Juice of ½ lemon

About 3 teaspoons olive oil

A few sprigs chives, chopped

1 red chili pepper, seeded and
finely chopped

Salt and freshly ground black pepper

6 slices bread (I like to use a hearty
bread), toasted

½ garlic clove

Seeds of 1 small pomegranate

A few sprigs cilantro, chopped

Halve and pit the avocados, then scoop out the flesh and place it in a mixing bowl. Immediately drizzle it with the lemon juice and smash roughly with a fork. Add the olive oil, then the chives and chili pepper and mix well. Season with salt and pepper.

Rub each slice of toast with the garlic clove and generously spread on the avocado mixture. Sprinkle with the pomegranate seeds and cilantro.

If you make the avocado spread more than an hour ahead of serving time, smooth the top of the mixture and drizzle it with a little additional lemon juice to help keep it from darkening. Cover with plastic wrap and place in the refrigerator until you're ready to assemble the tartines.

FOR THE SMOKED HADDOCK CHOWDER

1 stalk celery

1 yellow onion

2 tablespoons (30 g) butter

14 ounces (400 g) small potatoes, small red, white or a mixture

4 cups (1 L) clam or fish bouillon (infusion made with packets) or seafood stock

4 cups (1 L) milk

One 1¼-pound (600 g) haddock fillet, cut into 3 to 4 pieces, so they fit easily in the pan

1 head broccoli, florets only

2 yellow zucchini, sliced into rounds

One 10-ounce (300 g) can of corn, drained

1 cup (250 ml) heavy cream

1 bunch cilantro, washed and chopped

Finely slice the celery and onion. In a large pot over low heat, sauté the celery and onion in the butter until the onion is translucent, about 8 to 10 minutes. Slice the potatoes into thirds. Pour the bouillon into the pot and add the potatoes. Bring to a boil, cover with the lid, and allow to cook for about 15 minutes, or until the potatoes are soft. Meanwhile, bring the milk to a low boil in another pot, add the haddock pieces, and cook for 15 minutes to remove some of the salt. Remove the haddock pieces with a large slotted spoon and allow to cool. Remove the skin and flake the haddock into fairly large bite-sized pieces.

Bring a pot of salted water to a boil and cook the broccoli florets and zucchini slices for 5 minutes, then drain well.

Combine all the ingredients—broccoli, zucchini, corn, and haddock—with the bouillon and potatoes. Add the cream and stir well.

To thicken the soup, remove 2 or 3 ladlefuls, scooping out mainly potatoes and corn, and blend them, then return the smooth mixture to the soup. Just before serving, reheat the soup over low heat and scatter with the cilantro.

The chowder is a very practical recipe because it can be made at the spur of the moment. Smoked haddock is a fish that can be stored for a certain length of time. Since you'll already have most of the ingredients in your pantry, all you'll need to buy are the fresh vegetables.

LEEK "MAKI"
PORK TONKATSU
CRUNCHY COLESLAW

Yes, you can make tonkatsu at home for your guests! This beloved Japanese comfort food is actually not super complicated to make: you'll dip pork cutlets in beaten eggs, dredge them in light, crisp panko breadcrumbs, and deep-fry them. Served with leek maki, coleslaw and an ice cold beer, this is a bit of Tokyo at home.

TO SERVE 4

Note: Be sure to prepare the leeks and coleslaw before the tonkatsu, as you will want to serve it hot.

FOR THE LEEK MAKI

4 medium-sized leeks, white parts only

Fleur de sel and freshly ground pepper

Olive oil for drizzling

Balsamic vinegar for drizzling

Golden sesame seeds for garnish

Thoroughly wash the leeks and cut the white parts crosswise into pieces 1 to 1½ inches (3 to 4 cm) long, keeping them as even as possible. Cook in salted boiling water for about 15 minutes, testing for doneness with the tip of a knife—the leeks should be tender. Drain and allow to cool slightly. To serve, arrange them upright on a plate to look like maki. Season with Fleur de sel and pepper and drizzle a little olive oil and balsamic vinegar over the tops. Sprinkle generously with the golden sesame seeds.

FOR THE COLESLAW

2 medium-sized carrots, peeled	1 tablespoon mustard
½ head white cabbage	¼ cup (60 ml) plain yogurt
1 Granny Smith apple, unpeeled	3 tablespoons mayonnaise
1 tablespoon olive oil	Salt and freshly ground black pepper
3 tablespoons sherry vinegar	2 tablespoons raisins

Grate the carrots and slice the cabbage finely. Cut the apple into matchsticks. In a skillet, sauté the cabbage briefly in the olive oil, then deglaze the pan with the vinegar, scraping up any bits that have stuck to the bottom of the pan. Transfer to a salad bowl and add the carrots and apple. Make a dressing by stirring together the mustard, yogurt, mayonnaise, and raisins. Pour the dressing over the vegetables, mix well, and adjust the seasoning.

FOR THE PORK TONKATSU

One boneless pork loin	1 egg, lightly beaten
2½ cups (200 g) panko (Japanese breadcrumbs)	1¼ cups (300 ml) vegetable oil for frying
Salt and freshly ground black pepper	Tonkatsu sauce (available at Japanese grocery stores) for serving

Cut the loin into slices just under ½ inch (1 cm) thick and flatten each slice with the side of a wide knife. Season the panko with salt and pepper. Dip each slice of pork into the beaten egg and then coat with the panko crumbs.

In a large skillet, heat the oil until it registers 350°F (180°C) on a deep-fry thermometer and fry the slices of pork until golden. When large bubbles of oil no longer rise to the surface, the pork is cooked. Place the tonkatsu slices on sheets of paper towel to drain. Serve with tonkatsu sauce.

The slightly sinful feeling of eating fried food, the delicately sweet sauce, and the crunchy vegetables will delight all your guests, young and old. The adults will enjoy downing a well-chilled beer with this meal.

ZUCCHINI WITH MINT AND PINE NUTS
CALAMARI, CHICKPEAS, AND CHORIZO
SGROPPINO

This is another sensory discovery menu. The sautéed zucchini, with fresh mint and pine nuts, opens the way to a hardy calamari main course (and will likely become one of your go-to recipes). Finish with the freshest of desserts—a lemon sorbet whipped with vodka and prosecco and served ice cold.

TO SERVE 4

FOR THE ZUCCHINI

1 clove garlic

1 organic lemon

4 medium size zucchini

2 tablespoons pine nuts

¼ cup (60 ml) olive oil, plus more for drizzling

Salt and freshly ground black pepper

Leaves of a few sprigs mint, chopped

Peel and chop the garlic clove. Using a zester or a peeler, peel the skin off half of the lemon, eliminating any white pith, and squeeze the juice of the whole lemon. Finely chop the zest. Cut the zucchini into ¼-inch (5-mm) rounds. In a small skillet, toast the pine nuts until golden. In a larger skillet, heat the oil over medium heat heat and add the garlic, lemon zest, and zucchini. Cook for about 10 minutes, stirring frequently, then deglaze the skillet with the lemon juice. Season with salt and pepper and transfer to a serving dish. Just before serving, scatter the zucchini with the pine nuts and chopped mint leaves, and drizzle with a little olive oil.

FOR THE CALAMARI

16 ounces drained canned chickpeas

2¼ pounds (1 kg) small calamari, cleaned Note: ask your fish monger to do this

7 ounces (200 g) chorizo

¼ cup (60 ml) olive oil

2 cloves garlic, chopped

1 pinch Piment d'Espelette (a mild chili pepper from the Basque region) or other mild chili pepper

3 tablespoons sherry vinegar

1 bunch flat-leaf parsley, chopped

Salt and freshly ground pepper

Rinse the chickpeas. Clean the calamari and cut into strips, keeping the tentacles whole. Cut the chorizo into sticks. Heat the oil in a sauté pan over low heat and add the garlic. When it begins to color, add the chorizo and calamari. Increase the heat to high and fry the ingredients for 3 to 4 minutes, until the calamari flesh is opaque. Transfer the calamari and chorizo to a separate bowl and season with the Piment d'Espelette, salt, and pepper. Add the vinegar to the sauté pan and bring to the boil, then allow to reduce for 3 minutes. Return the calamari and chorizo to the pan, add the chickpeas to heat them, and toss well. Transfer to a warm serving dish and sprinkle with the chopped parsley.

Note: You can enhance this recipe by using home-cooked chickpeas. Soak them overnight beforehand and then cook according to the directions on the package.

FOR THE SGROPPINO

4 scoops lemon sorbet

⅔ cup (150 ml) vodka

½ bottle prosecco

An hour ahead of time, place a mixing bowl in the freezer so that it is well chilled when you need it. Whisk the sorbet, vodka, and prosecco together until the mixture is foamy. Quickly fill tall glasses and serve immediately.

LEMON-SCENTED VEAL SCALOPPINI
BRAISED ARTICHOKES

The combination of lemony veal scaloppini and the earthy taste of sautéed artichokes with a parmesan-breadcrumb topping is a perfect way to update this veal classic. I like to serve it with lemon wedges and a chilled white wine.

TO SERVE 4

FOR THE BRAISED ARTICHOKES

8 baby artichokes

Juice of 1 lemon

1 clove garlic

A few sprigs flat-leaf parsley

¼ cup (60 ml) olive oil

Salt and freshly ground pepper

Scant ½ cup (100 ml) water

2 ounces (50 g) Parmigiano, grated (about ¼ cup)

2 tablespoons breadcrumbs

Trim the artichoke stalks to just under ½ inch (1 cm) from the base. Remove the hard outer leaves and cut off at least one-third of the upper half of the top of each artichoke. Halve them and, using a paring knife, remove the fuzzy choke. Place in a mixing bowl, pour in the lemon juice, and add enough water to cover them, to keep them from turning brown. Soak for 15 minutes and drain. Peel and chop the garlic and chop the parsley leaves. Heat the oil in a sauté pan. Add the garlic, parsley, and artichokes and sauté over medium-high heat until golden. Season with salt and pepper and pour in the scant ½ cup (100 ml) water. Reduce the heat to low and cook for 30 minutes, stirring from time to time.

Combine the Parmigiano with the breadcrumbs and sprinkle the mixture over the artichokes in the pan. Cook for 5 minutes more and serve.

FOR THE SCALOPPINI

1 organic or unwaxed lemon

1 sprig lemon verbena

8 small, thin veal scaloppini

Salt and freshly ground pepper

2 tablespoons olive oil

3 tablespoons (50 g) butter, diced

1 lemon cut into wedges, for serving

Grate the zest of the lemon and juice it. Pick the leaves off the sprig of lemon verbena. Season the scaloppini with salt and pepper. Cook them in a heated skillet with the olive oil for 3 to 4 minutes on each side. Transfer the meat to a serving dish.

Deglaze the pan juices and brown bits with the lemon juice and allow to reduce. Stir in the lemon zest and add the butter in several additions, stirring more in only when the butter in the pan has melted.

Pour the sauce over the scaloppini and garnish with the lemon slices and lemon verbena leaves.

TREVISO SALAD WITH ANCHOVIES
OCTOPUS, POTATOES, AND PIMENTÓN
ESPRESSO AFFOGATO

A crunchy treviso salad with a warm anchovy-sherry vinaigrette followed by delicious poached octopus, served on a bed of smoky paprika potatoes, celery, and red onion, makes a delightful summer lunch or dinner menu. "Dessert" is an espresso served with a small scoop of vanilla gelato. Bravo!

TO SERVE 6

FOR THE TREVISO SALAD

1 or 2 heads radicchio lettuce, depending on their size

⅓ cup (90 ml) olive oil

2 cloves garlic, chopped

6 anchovies, packed in oil

3 tablespoons (45 ml) sherry vinegar

Wash the radicchio. Cut the large leaves into pieces but keep the smaller ones whole. Place all of the leaves in a salad bowl.

To make the vinaigrette, heat the oil in a small skillet over low heat and add the garlic and anchovies. The anchovies will disintegrate when exposed to heat. Increase the heat and add the vinegar, which will evaporate as it cooks. Remove the skillet from the heat, pour the hot vinaigrette over the radicchio leaves, and serve.

FOR THE OCTOPUS

2¼ pounds (1 kg) octopus, or several small octopuses

1½ pounds (750 g) medium-sized potatoes

1 spring or small red onion

1 bunch flat-leaf parsley

2 stalks celery

Olive oil

Juice of 1 lemon

1 tablespoon pimentón or smoked paprika

Salt and freshly ground black pepper

Begin by cleaning the octopus: first turn the hood inside out and slice it off, then remove the eyes and the beak at the base of the hood. You may also ask your fish monger to clean them.

Place the octopus in a large pot and cover with cold water. Bring to a boil and cook for 40 minutes. The octopus is done when a knife inserted into the meat slides in as easily as if it were softened butter. Allow the octopus to cool in the cooking water.

Meanwhile, bring a pot of salted water to a boil and cook the potatoes for 15 minutes. When they are tender, cut them into fairly thick slices. Rinse the octopus under running water, remove the skin, and cut the meat into bite-size pieces leaving tentacles a bit longer. Chop the spring onion, roughly chop the flat-leaf parsley, and cut the celery into small pieces.

Combine all of these ingredients in a bowl, season with the olive oil and lemon juice, and then with salt and pepper. Sprinkle evenly with pimentón. Transfer to a serving platter.

This dish may be eaten either still warm or at room temperature.

Another version of the recipe calls for cooking the octopus in a court-bouillon, with the classic aromatics of carrot, celery, onion, and bouquet garni. If you opt for this method, the octopus will be even tastier.

FOR THE ESPRESSO AFFOGATO

For each person, prepare one serving of espresso coffee. Place a scoop of vanilla ice cream in a sturdy glass, add a dash of amaretto, and pour over the hot coffee. Serve immediately, adding roasted sliced almonds or crumbled almond cookies, depending on your preference.

CREAMY CELERIAC SOUP WITH SAGE BUTTER
SCALLOPS
HARICOT BEANS

This is another meal that looks more difficult and exotic than it actually is, so I encourage you to try it sooner than later. The delicate yet hardy taste of the celery root soup, garnished with crispy sage leaves, paves the way to a perfect combination of sautéed scallops, with a hint of Piment Espelette, served with herb-infused white beans.

A real winner—you will deserve the inevitable bravos from your guests!

TO SERVE 6

FOR THE SOUP

For the soup

2 tablespoons butter

1 yellow onion, chopped

4 potatoes, peeled and diced into approximately 1½-inch pieces

1 celeriac, peeled and cut into approximately 1½-inch pieces

4 cups (1L) chicken stock

200 ml whipping cream

Salt and freshly ground black pepper

Melt the butter in a pot over medium heat. Add the onion and sweat it for 3 minutes. Add the potatoes, celeriac, and chicken stock. Bring to a boil, cover with the lid, and simmer for 20 minutes, or until the vegetables have softened. Remove from the heat and process with an immersion blender until smooth. Stir in the cream and season with salt and pepper.

You can take soup off the heat and reheat over a low heat just before serving.

FOR THE SAGE-SCENTED BROWNED BUTTER

3 tablespoons (50 g) butter

15 fresh sage leaves

Melt the butter in a saucepan. Fry the sage leaves in the butter until crisp; the butter should be slightly browned. Drizzle a little of the browned butter (in French, it is known as *beurre noisette*, or hazelnut butter) over the hot soup and scatter with the sage leaves.

FOR THE SCALLOPS

24 scallops, cleaned

2 tablespoons (30 g) butter

Maldon salt

Crushed Piment d'Espelette (a mild chili pepper from the Basque region of France) or other mild chili pepper

Rinse the scallops and trim any remaining gray parts. Pat them dry with sheets of paper towel. Melt the butter in a skillet over high heat and cook the scallops for 2 minutes on each side, until golden. Serve immediately with a small pinch of Piment d'Espelette and a few grains of Maldon salt on each scallop.

FOR THE HARICOT BEANS

2¼ pounds (1 kg) fresh white beans in their pods (we use cocos de Paimpol, a semi-dried bean). Note: if using dried beans, quantity is 500 g or 1 pound)

1 garlic clove

1 onion

1 bouquet garni (sage, thyme, and bay leaf)

3 tablespoons olive oil

Salt and freshly ground black pepper

A few sprigs flat-leaf parsley, chopped

Shell the cocos de Paimpol beans and put them along with the garlic, onion, and bouquet garni in a pot large enough that there is about 2 inches of water over the beans. Bring to a low medium boil, add salt and a drizzle of olive oil, and cook for 25 minutes. Test for doneness by tasting regularly. You can also use dry beans, which are just as delicious but take longer to cook—about 45 minutes, depending on the variety. Simply soak them overnight in cold water before cooking. Rinse and cook them in the same way as above, making sure to allow at least 45 minutes cooking time, and testing regularly for doneness after 30 minutes.

Using a large slotted spoon, transfer the cooked beans to a serving bowl. Discard the aromatic ingredients with the exception of the garlic clove, which you should crush in a salad bowl. Combine with the remaining olive oil, season with salt and pepper to taste, and stir in the beans and parsley.

Serve warm with the scallops.

Helpful Hint: These tasty beans may be served as a side with other dishes, but in my opinion, this surf and turf combination is particularly succulent. They are also delicious chilled and accompanied with a drizzle of vinegar.

WEEKEND AND HOLIDAY MENUS

LEEKS MIMOSA WITH VINAIGRETTE
VEAL STEW IN TOMATO SAUCE

You can add leeks to the list of vegetables that we too often forget. Veal sauté, or stew, is another traditional French dish that will make your guests feel as if they are in a beloved neighborhood bistro in Paris. Be sure to allow enough time for the veal to cook slowly, so it becomes super tender.

TO SERVE 4

FOR THE LEEKS MIMOSA

4 medium leeks

1 egg, hard boiled

2 tablespoons Dijon mustard

¼ cup (60 ml) sunflower seed oil

Salt and freshly ground black pepper

1 tablespoon sherry vinegar

Thoroughly wash the leeks and cut off the green parts. Remove the outer layer of the leeks and cut each leek into 2 or 3 pieces, depending on their length. Cook them in a large pot of salted boiling water for about 15 minutes, until tender. Drain and allow to cool.

Peel and chop the hard-boiled egg as finely as possible. Prepare a thick vinaigrette: whisk the mustard and oil together with salt and pepper to taste, then whisk in the vinegar.

Divide the leeks among four plates. Drizzle with the vinaigrette and sprinkle with the chopped egg.

Serve at room temperature or slightly chilled (chopped egg topping should always be at room temperature).

Note: This may be prepared ahead of time and dressed just before serving.

FOR THE VEAL STEW

3 pounds (1.5 kg) stewing veal

2 medium yellow onions

2 carrots

1 stalk celery

8 ounces (225 g) white mushrooms

Olive oil

1 tablespoon all-purpose flour

2 garlic cloves, peeled

1 bouquet garni (sage, thyme, and bay leaf)

1 tablespoon tomato paste

1 small glass white wine

2 cups (500 ml) vegetable stock

Salt and freshly ground black pepper

Ask your butcher to cut the meat into 2-inch (5-cm) cubes, or cut it yourself. Peel and chop the onions. Peel the carrots and celery stalk and slice them. In a large pot, heat a little olive oil and lightly sauté the onions, carrots, and celery. Add the meat and allow the pieces to brown, turning them until they have browned all over. Sprinkle the flour into the pot and mix thoroughly. Add the garlic cloves and bouquet garni and stir in the tomato paste. Deglaze with the white wine, scraping up any brown bits that stick to the bottom of the pan. Stir again, then pour in the vegetable stock. Cover the pot with the lid and simmer gently over low heat for 30 minutes. Wash the mushrooms and quarter them. Add the mushrooms and continue to simmer for an additional 30 minutes. Season with salt and pepper and serve accompanied with brown rice.

Note: The veal stew may also be prepared the night before.

PASTA ALLA NORMA

A classic Sicilian pasta featuring tomatoes, eggplant, and ricotta salata named after the composer Vincenzo Bellini's opera Norma. Every cook needs some go-to pasta dishes and this can easily become one to add to your repertoire. Serve with a simple rocket salad seasoned with lemon juice, olive oil, salt and freshly ground black pepper, and topped with shaved Parmesan. A glass of red wine and you are set!

TO SERVE 4

2 large eggplants

Olive oil

1 garlic clove, peeled and finely chopped

Leaves of 1 bunch basil

1 teaspoon dried oregano

1 pound (450 g) whole peeled tomatoes, or 2 cups (500 ml) passata (uncooked tomato purée)

A little white wine vinegar, about 1 teaspoon

Salt and freshly ground black pepper

1 pound (450 g) dry penne

5 ounces (150 g) ricotta salata or pecorino, grated (about 1 cup)

Cut each eggplant lengthwise into 4 pieces. Then cut the pieces widthwise to make large cubes. Preheat the oven on the broil setting. Arrange the eggplant cubes in a baking dish and drizzle generously with olive oil, mixing with your hands to ensure that all the pieces are well coated. Place the baking dish in the middle of the oven and broil for at least 20 minutes, turning them over halfway through the cooking process, until nicely golden all over.

While the eggplant bakes, drizzle a little olive oil in a large skillet and sauté the garlic with the basil leaves (set some of the smaller leaves aside for garnish). Add the tomatoes and oregano and adjust the heat to low, and allow the liquid to reduce for about 15 minutes. Season with salt and pepper and add a dash of white wine vinegar. Lastly, stir the finished eggplant cubes into the sauce and cook for an additional 10 minutes.

In a large pot of salted boiling water, cook the pasta according to the directions on the package. When the penne are al dente, drain them in a colander, reserving a little of the cooking liquid. Return the pasta to the pot and place over medium low heat and immediately add the sauce, as well as 2 tablespoons of the reserved cooking liquid, and mix well. Scatter with the reserved basil leaves, grated cheese, and a last dash of olive oil.

ROASTED GREEN ASPARAGUS
SUMMER OSSO BUCCO

———————

A lighter version of the classic osso bucco thanks to the fennel and lemons that cook with the veal shanks. Serve with roasted asparagus, and you and your guests will welcome the long summer evenings enjoying this Italian classic.

TO SERVE 6

FOR THE OSSO BUCO

2 yellow onions	4 fennel bulbs
Leaves of 1 sprig rosemary, chopped	2 organic or unwaxed lemons, thinly sliced
¼ cup (60 ml) olive oil	2 tablespoons powdered veal stock
2 veal shanks, each cut into 3 slices	¼ cup capers packed in salt

Peel and chop the onions. In a heavy ovenproof pot or Dutch oven over medium heat, sauté the onions and rosemary with 2 tablespoons of the olive oil until the onions are translucent. Remove from the pot, add the remaining 2 tablespoons of olive oil, and sear the meat slices for 5 minutes on each side. When they are nicely browned, return the onions and rosemary to the pot.

Preheat the oven to 375°F (190°C).

Wash the fennel bulbs, remove the outer layer, and quarter them. Remove the meat slices from the pot and make a layer of fennel quarters over the onions, then add a few lemon slices. Sprinkle with 1 tablespoon of the powdered veal stock. Arrange the meat slices over this layer and season them with salt and pepper. Cover with a layer of lemon slices and sprinkle with the remaining veal stock. Cover the pot and place it in the oven for 1 hour 15 minutes. Ten minutes before the time is up, rinse and drain the capers and add them to the pot, stirring the ingredients.

If you wish, you can prolong the cooking time in the oven. Reduce the temperature to 225°F (110°C) and cook for a further 30 minutes or so. This will ensure that the meat is even more tender.

For the asparagus

2 bunches green asparagus

Olive oil

Salt and freshly ground black pepper

Balsamic vinegar, for drizzling

Parmigiano shavings, for finishing

Preheat the oven to 375°F (190°C).

Wash the asparagus and cut off the hard bottoms. Place them on a rimmed baking tray and drizzle them with olive oil. Season with salt and pepper and roast in the oven for about 20 minutes, or until the tips just begin to darken.

Serve when still warm, drizzled with a little balsamic vinegar and scattered with Parmigiano shavings.

CREAMY BELL PEPPER SOUP
SALAD NIÇOISE
NEAPOLITAN RICOTTA CAKE

The chilled bell pepper soup is a tasty starter that paves the way for the crunchy salad niçoise.

The tarte Gennà, a Napoletano dessert known as the migliaccio, was made for me by my friend Gennaro and I'm wild about it. It's a popular cake that combines the texture of a custard flan with the intensity of citrus flavors. And if you have any left over, it'll be even better for breakfast the next day. Gennaro was kind enough to share his secret recipe with me.

Have fun with your table décor and use a color theme that complements the colors of the meal. Here I have used an African Dutch wax fabric in green and yellow that I ordered online and have mixed with pottery plates, Mexican water glasses and vintage French glass soup bowls.

TO SERVE 6

FOR THE CREAMY BELL PEPPER SOUP

2 fresh red and 2 yellow bell peppers, or 2 jars of peeled bell peppers (16 oz / 500 g) drained, plus more for garnish

2 yellow onions

2 cloves garlic

Scant ½ cup (100 ml) olive oil

Scant ½ cup (100 g) white rice

1 bouquet garni

1 cup (250 g) mascarpone

2 teaspoons paprika

1 pinch Piment d'Espelette or other mild chili pepper

Salt and freshly ground black pepper

If you are using fresh bell peppers, wash them and place them under a preheated broiler for 20 minutes, turning them frequently. Transfer them to a re-cycled plastic or paper bag and allow to cool; this will enable you to remove the skin easily by hand. If necessary, use a small paring knife to scrape off any excess charred areas. Remove the peels, seeds, and any pith and cut them into pieces.

If you have opted to save time and use jarred bell peppers, drain them and cut them into large pieces. Peel and dice the onions and garlic. Drizzle some of the olive oil into a large pot and place it over low heat. Add the onions and garlic and let them cook until softened, about 5 minutes. Add the bell peppers and continue cooking, stirring constantly. Pour in 4 cups (1 liter) water and bring to a simmer, then add the rice and the bouquet garni. Cover and simmer for 20 minutes over low heat.

Remove the bouquet garni and purée with an immersion blender or food processer (in batches if necessary) until smooth, gradually incorporating the mascarpone and remaining olive oil. Transfer to a bowl and season with the paprika and Piment d'Espelette. Let cool, then refrigerate until well chilled.

Serve garnished with diced bell peppers of different colors.

FOR THE SALAD NIÇOISE

1 clove garlic

10 – 12 cooked baby potatoes, peeled and still warm, red or white potatoes or a mix

Mixed salad greens

7 ounces (200 g) fresh green beans, cooked but crunchy

1 red bell pepper and 1 green bell pepper, seeds and pith removed, sliced into long slivers

1 celery heart, cut on an angle into slices

1 bunch radishes, cut in half lengthwise

1 fennel bulb, sliced

1 pound (450 g) drained oil-packed tuna

6 hard-boiled eggs, peeled and cut in half

7 ounces (200 g) fresh fava beans, blanched and peeled

12 anchovy fillets packed in oil

20 pitted black olives, cut in half

2 spring onions, sliced into rounds

Salt and freshly ground black pepper

High-quality olive oil

A few basil leaves

Slice the garlic clove in half lengthwise and rub the serving platter or bowl with it. Halve the potatoes, arrange them on the base of the platter, and drizzle with a little olive oil. Arrange a bed of mixed salad greens around the potato halves, and continue with the other vegetables, positioning them to make an attractive display. Top with large pieces of tuna, alternating them with the hard-boiled egg halves, each topped with an anchovy. Scatter the olives and sliced spring onions over the top and season with salt and pepper.

Pour a generous glug of olive oil over all of the ingredients and garnish with the basil leaves. But no vinegar! It would overpower the taste of the fresh raw vegetables.

FOR THE RICOTTA CAKE

3 cups (75 cl) water

2 cups (50 cl) milk

1 pinch salt

3 tablespoons (50 g) butter, plus more for the tart pan

8 ounces (250 g) durum wheat fine semolina

1 lemon, unwaxed or organic

1 orange, unwaxed or organic

2½ cups (500 g) sugar

2 cups (500 g) whole-milk ricotta

5 eggs

Confectioners' sugar for dusting

In a large heavy pot, bring the water, milk, salt, and butter to the boil. Pour in the semolina, whisking to prevent lumps from forming. Cook for 5 to 8 minutes, whisking constantly, then remove from the heat and allow to cool.

Preheat the oven to 350°F (180°C) and grease a tart pan with butter.

Grate the lemon and orange for zest and set aside. Whisk or stir the sugar, ricotta, and eggs together and stir in the grated zest, so that the mixture is smooth and creamy. Combine the ricotta mixture with the semolina. The mixture should resemble a thick liquid. Pour the mixture into the prepared tart pan. Bake for about 1 hour, until the tart is a nice golden brown, then remove from oven and allow to cool. As this is more like a flan, but more dense, 1 hour cooking time is sufficient.

Dust the top of the cake with a little confectioners' sugar, sifted through a fine-mesh sieve, and serve at room temperature.

SAFFRON-SCENTED RISOTTO WITH MUSSELS
ORANGE SALAD WITH FENNEL

_____

For this menu, the classic Milanese saffron risotto is revisited and partnered with mussels. Begin your meal with a Sicilian staple, an orange-and-fennel salad with Kalamata olives and capers that will surprise your guests and make them smile.

SERVES 4 TO 6

FOR THE RISOTTO

2¼ pounds (1 kg) mussels

6 cups (1.5 liters) fish stock

1 yellow onion, finely chopped

1 stalk celery, finely sliced

14 ounces (400 g) Arborio rice (about 2 cups)

1 small glass dry white wine

½ teaspoon saffron threads

1 cup boiling water

5 tablespoons (70 g) butter

3½ ounces (100 g) mascarpone (scant ½ cup)

Salt and freshly ground black pepper

Wash and brush the mussels and place them in a large pot over high heat. Cover and allow them to cook until they open, stirring occasionally. This should take about 10 minutes. Allow them to cool and remove them from their shells, leaving a few in their shells for decoration.

To make the risotto, follow the same directions as those given in the Risotto Primavera (page 59); simply replace the chicken or vegetable stock with shellfish stock.

Place the saffron threads in a bowl, cover with the boiling water, and allow to infuse for 10 minutes. When you make the risotto, combine the saffron-infused water with the last ladleful of stock that you add to the pan. Lastly, add the mussels to the rice and stir in the butter and mascarpone. Remove from the heat, cover, and allow to rest for 2 minutes, then serve.

FOR THE SALAD

4 organic oranges

2 fennel bulbs, thinly sliced, and fronds reserved

About 15 black olives, pitted and halved (I like to use Kalamata or Niçoise olives)

Juice of ½ lemon

Scant ⅓ cup (75 ml) olive oil

A few leaves flat-leaf parsley, chopped

A sprinkle of pepperoncino

Salt and freshly ground black pepper

Peel the oranges carefully, removing all the white pith, and, working over a salad bowl to collect the juice, slice them into thin rounds. Arrange them in a circular pattern on a serving platter, alternating them with the fennel slices. Scatter the olives over the salad with the chopped parsley.

To make the dressing, combine the lemon juice, orange juice, and olive oil, and season with pepperoncino, salt, and pepper. Mix together to form an emulsion and drizzle evenly over the salad.

I like to prepare the salad first, as the risotto requires more attention to finish.

BELGIAN ENDIVE SALAD WITH PEARS AND BLUE CHEESE
DUCK BREAST À L'ORANGE
HONEY-GLAZED TURNIPS

A crunchy endive, pear, and green grape salad with a crumbled blue cheese dressing, followed by tender duck breasts with a hint of orange zest and accompanied by honey-sautéed turnips, works perfectly for a weekend dinner or a leisurely Sunday lunch. Serve with crunchy, warm French bread and a glass of white or red Burgundy. Instead of a classic dessert, I like to surprise my guests with a selection of cheeses served with dried fruit, candied quince paste, and fruit jams.

Et voilà!

TO SERVE 4

FOR THE BELGIAN ENDIVE SALAD

3 Belgian endives

10 hazelnuts

1 small bunch large green grapes

1 pear

5 ounces (150 g) blue cheese, such as Roquefort, fourme d'Ambert, or Stilton

3 tablespoons olive oil

1 tablespoon sherry vinegar

Salt and freshly ground black pepper

Remove and discard the outer leaves of the endives and slice them lengthwise, making sure to keep the small leaves whole. Chop the hazelnuts, cut the grapes in half, and slice the pear. Combine the ingredients in a salad bowl. Crumble half of the cheese into the bowl. To prepare the dressing, mash the remaining blue cheese and mix it into the oil and vinegar, seasoning it with salt and pepper. Pour the dressing over the salad, toss carefully, and serve.

FOR THE DUCK BREASTS

2 large duck breasts

½ unwaxed or organic orange, juiced, with peel finely chopped or grated

4 tablespoons honey

Salt and freshly ground black pepper

Begin heating a skillet. Using a sharp knife, make several incisions in the skin of each breast in a criss-cross pattern (be careful not to cut into the flesh). When the skillet is nice and hot, sear the duck breasts skin side down. Cook for about 15 minutes, spooning off the fat as it melts. Turn the duck breasts over and cook briefly, about 3 minutes. Remove from the skillet and allow them to rest under aluminum foil for 10 minutes.

Cut each breast widthwise into 6 slices. The skillet should still be hot: pour in the honey and then the orange juice and zest, and return to low heat. Stir until the ingredients come together smoothly to form a sauce. Place the duck slices on a serving platter and pour the sauce over them. Serve the duck breast slices hot with the caramelized sauce, accompanied by the caramelized turnips.

FOR THE TURNIPS

2¼ pounds (1 kg) small turnips

2 tablespoons butter

3 tablespoons honey

Salt and freshly ground pepper

Peel and trim the turnips, leaving about ½ inch (1 cm) of the green stems. Halve any large turnips. Place them in a pot and half-cover with water. Cook over a medium heat until the water has evaporated and the turnips are tender but not too soft, usually about 15 minutes. Reduce the heat and melt the butter in the pot to coat them. Stir in the honey, season with salt and pepper, and allow the turnips to caramelize gently before serving.

Note: Turnips may be prepared ahead of time, saving the final step of the honey glaze until just before serving with the duck.

Instead of a classic dessert, I like to surprise my guests with a selection of cheeses served with dried fruit, candied quince paste, and fruit jams.

ASPARAGUS VICHYSSOISE
VITELLO TONNATO

When you have the time to treat your guests to a special meal, a summer lunch or dinner for special guests, take the time to prepare this menu. This is really a confidence builder for any home cook as it is a delicious and impressive meal. The creamy, cool asparagus vichyssoise is fresh and has a delicate yet hardy flavor and the vitello tonnato is a complete explosion of flavor.

TO SERVE 6

FOR THE VICHYSSOISE

1 bunch green asparagus

10 ounces (300 g) leeks, white parts only

½ yellow onion

1 pound (450 g) potatoes (such as Yukon Golds)

1 tablespoon (20 g) butter

4 cups (1 liter) chicken stock: homemade or organic

Salt and freshly ground black pepper

⅔ cup (150 ml) crème fraîche

1 pinch freshly grated nutmeg

Snap off the bottoms of the asparagus spears, then cut off the tips and reserve them. Cut the asparagus stems into small pieces. Wash and peel the leeks and potatoes, and peel the onions. Cut these vegetables into small pieces.

Melt the butter in a large pot or Dutch oven and sauté the leeks, onions, and asparagus pieces without allowing them to brown. Add the chicken stock and potatoes and season with salt and pepper. Bring the liquid to a boil. While the water is boiling, briefly cook the asparagus tips (for about 2 minutes), which should remain al dente, then remove them with a slotted spoon and set them aside for serving.

Let the soup cook over medium heat for 30 minutes. Remove from heat, then process or blend it, adding in the crème fraîche. Return the puréed soup to the pot to reheat for 5 minutes, but do not allow it to boil. Stir in a pinch of ground nutmeg. Remove from the heat and allow to cool, then chill.

Serve chilled, decorated with the asparagus tips.

FOR THE VITELLO TONNATO
TO COOK THE VEAL

1 carrot

1 yellow onion

2 whole cloves

1 stalk celery

1 bouquet garni (a few sprigs of parsley and 2 bay leaves tied together)

1 small glass white wine

One 1½-pound (700 g) veal roast

FOR THE SAUCE

7 ounces (200 g) drained oil-packed tuna

6 anchovies packed in oil

1 hard-boiled egg

1 tablespoon sherry vinegar

1 cup mayonnaise

3 handfuls arugula, washed and dried

1 tablespoon capers, rinsed and drained

Salt and freshly ground black pepper

Peel the carrot and onion and stud the onion with the cloves. Place the carrot and onion in a large pot or Dutch oven with the celery stalk and the bouquet garni, and pour in the white wine. Add enough water so that the pan is ¾ full and bring to a boil. Place the veal in the pot, cover, simmer over low heat for 30 minutes, and allow to cool in the pot.

To make the sauce, process or blend the tuna, anchovies, egg, vinegar, and 2 tablespoons of the veal cooking broth, or more to thin if necessary. The sauce should be smooth. Incorporate the mayonnaise and adjust the salt and pepper if necessary.

Remove the veal from the pot and slice very thinly. Make a bed of arugula leaves on the serving platter and arrange the veal slices over it. Drop spoonfuls of tuna sauce over the meat and scatter the capers on top.

Note: If you know your butcher, you can ask him to slice the cooked veal roast by machine.

Allow the dish to chill in the refrigerator before serving; 30 minutes is fine.

SERVING COFFEE AFTER A MEAL

Do you remember when you last enjoyed coffee that was served stylishly at the dining table, or once you have retired to the living room?

Make it as it should be prepared, with a filter machine or a stovetop espresso maker, and turn your post-meal coffee into a veritable ceremony by presenting it in an attractive coffee service (I found the one shown here at a Paris flea market). If you choose delicate cookies to accompany your coffee, it becomes a course that can replace dessert.

FENNEL AND MUSHROOM SALAD WITH PARMIGIANO REGGIANO
PROVENÇAL BRAISED BEEF STEW
VANILLA ICE CREAM WITH OLIVE OIL AND FLEUR DE SEL

———————

Treat your friends or family to this weekend feast. You can assemble the main dish the evening before and leave it in the refrigerator to marinate overnight, then slowly cook it over low heat the day of your dinner party. The best part is that the leftover beef stew makes the best pasta sauce, which you can enjoy during the week, or freeze to use when you have nothing in the pantry.

My friends with children swear by this dish: they serve this meltingly tender braised beef with potatoes or over pasta, accompanied by a simple mixed-green salad. And the easy dessert will surely be copied by all of your guests.

TO SERVE 6

FOR THE SALAD

For the salad

About 10 medium-sized fresh mushrooms

2 fennel bulbs

Juice of 1 lemon

5 tablespoons or a scant 1/3 cup virgin olive oil

Salt and freshly ground black pepper

Parmigiano shavings for garnish

Wash the mushrooms, slightly trimming the bottoms of the stems, then pat them dry on paper towels and slice them. Cut off the fennel stalks, reserving the best green fronds for decoration. Using a paring knife, remove the outer skin and the hard base of the fennel bulbs. Using a sharp mandoline (be sure not to get your fingers too close to the blade!), slice the bulbs into a serving bowl. Add the sliced mushrooms to the bowl. Whisk together the lemon juice, olive oil, and salt and pepper to taste to make an emulsion. Just before serving, pour the dressing over the salad, gently toss the fennel and mushrooms, and dot the cheese shavings on the top.

FOR THE BRAISED BEEF STEW

A daube de boeuf is a classic Provençal braised beef dish, slightly different from its northern relative, the boeuf bourguignon.

2 pounds (1 kg) stewing beef, such as chuck

5 ounces (150 g) smoked bacon, cut into matchsticks

3 carrots, sliced into rounds

3 onions, chopped

1 10-ounce (250 g) can peeled tomatoes

3 garlic cloves, crushed

5 ounces (150 g) green and black olives, pitted

2 cups (500 ml) dry white wine

Scant ½ cup (100 ml) olive oil

Zest of 1 unwaxed or organic orange

1 bouquet garni (bay leaf, rosemary, and thyme)

Salt and freshly ground black pepper

A day ahead, cut the meat into large cubes. Line the bottom of a large, heavy pot with the bacon and then place the beef, carrots, onions, tomatoes, garlic, and olives on top. Pour in the white wine and olive oil (the beef and vegetables should be covered), then add the orange zest and bouquet garni. Season with salt and pepper.

Allow to marinate overnight, covered, in the refrigerator. Leave yourself enough time to cook the stew well before serving, placing the covered pot over low heat and cooking for at least 5 hours. Be sure to check once every hour to be sure there is enough liquid in the pan and that the temperature is not too high.

Serve with boiled potatoes or small elbow macaroni (in France, there are known as coquillettes, or "little shells"), which will soak up the delicious sauce.

FOR THE DESSERT

Place scoops of vanilla ice cream in ice cream bowls and drizzle with a little fine-quality extra virgin olive oil. Sprinkle each serving with a dash of Fleur de sel and accompany with amaretti cookies for a final sweet touch.

And, most important, as soon as your guests have tasted this surprising dessert, quiz them to see if they can identify the ingredients.

TAGLIATELLE AL RAGÙ
CRUNCHY MIXED VEGETABLE SALAD

Trust me, this menu could just as easily be called "leftover heaven!" You might find yourself making the Provençal Braised Beef (page 149) just so you can turn the leftovers into this hearty ragôut with pasta. You can select your ingredients for the mixed salad from whatever's available at the market; what's important is for the salad to be colorful, crunchy, and refreshing.

TO SERVE 4 – 6

FOR THE TAGLIATELLE AL RAGÙ

Leftover braised Provençal beef with its sauce (page 149)

5 ounces (150 g) dried tagliatelle (per person)

A few sprigs of flat-leaf parsley, finely chopped

A little olive oil for drizzling

Grated Parmigiano for serving

If your guests haven't devoured every morsel of the braised beef and mopped up all its sauce, freeze the leftovers. When I prepare the daube, I tend to make more than required, because I know only too well that it can be enjoyed again on a day when I don't feel like cooking.

Reheat the leftover beef and sauce, then shred the beef into pieces small enough to easily incorporate into the sauce.

Cook the pasta according to package directions and drain. Pour the meat sauce over the pasta and sprinkle with the parsley. Drizzle with a little olive oil and add as much grated cheese as you like.

FOR THE CRUNCHY MIXED VEGETABLE SALAD

2 small Persian cucumbers or 1 medium size cucumber

8 – 10 cherry tomatoes

1 carrot

1 small fennel bulb

1 celery stalk

250g mixed salad greens

Olive oil and white wine vinegar

Salt and freshly ground black pepper

Wash and cut all of the vegetables as you think best (thin slices, cubes, shavings, rounds, torn, etc.). Combine in a salad bowl and dress with the olive oil and wine vinegar to taste—or dress the salad directly at the table if you have an oil and vinegar cruet set. Season with salt and pepper.

POULE AU POT
POACHED VEGETABLES

Poule au pot, or literally, "chicken in a pot," is a classic French dish consisting of poached chicken, vegetables, and an herb green sauce that you'll want to prepare on a weekend, when you have time to enjoy leisurely cooking and setting a more elaborate table. Save it for a special occasion with special guests, or as a special meal for your family. It is delicious, light, and unforgettable, and the leftovers make an incredible second meal!

I always ask a guest to bring dessert; in this case, a sinful chocolate tart from my favorite patisserie.

TO SERVE 6

FOR THE CHICKEN AND ITS BOULLION

1 4½ pound (2 kg) chicken or boiling fowl

1 stalk celery

A few sprigs flat-leaf parsley

1 onion, studded with a few cloves

2 garlic cloves, peeled

10 black peppercorns

1 bouquet garni (thyme, bay leaf)

2 carrots, peeled and left whole

AUTHOR'S SUGGESTION FOR INGREDIENTS TO ADD A "TWIST" TO THE TRADITIONAL RECIPE:

1 piece fresh ginger

2 small bird's eye chili peppers

Place the chicken in a large pot and pour in enough cold water to cover it. Bring it to a boil, regularly skimming off the cooking foam from the surface. Using kitchen twine, tie up the celery stalk with the parsley sprigs. Add all the aromatic ingredients that will flavor the broth as it cooks: the studded onion, garlic cloves, peppercorns, ginger, bird's eye chili peppers, the bundle of celery and parsley sprigs, the bouquet garni, and carrots. Allow to simmer for 1½ to 2 hours with the lid half on. Remove the chicken from the pot and keep it warm in a little of the broth. Discard all the aromatic ingredients, including carrots, and strain the broth through a fine-mesh sieve into a bowl; reserve.

FOR THE POACHED VEGETABLES

1 bunch carrots

½ celeriac

1 bunch turnips

3 parsnips

About 10 new potatoes

6 small leeks

About 10 brussels sprouts

1 small head Romanesco cauliflower

Reserved broth from poaching the chicken

Peel the carrots, celeriac, turnips (leaving 2 inches of green stem), parsnips, and potatoes. Trim the leeks, brussels sprouts, and cauliflower, then quarter the head of cauliflower. Cook the potatoes separately in water so that they don't cloud the broth. Cook the rest of the vegetables in the broth, starting with those that take the longest to cook, until all are fork-tender, about 15 minutes total. When ready to serve, remove the vegetables with a large slotted spoon and arrange them on a platter around the poached chicken.

While the vegetables are cooking, prepare the green sauce.

FOR THE GREEN SAUCE

1 tablespoon capers packed in salt, rinsed

6 gherkins

1 bunch flat-leaf parsley, leaves only

1 bunch tarragon, leaves only

3 tablespoons old-fashioned grainy

mustard

⅓ cup (75 ml) sunflower seed oil

2 tablespoons red wine vinegar

Salt and freshly ground black pepper

Chop the capers, gherkins, parsley, and tarragon with a knife. Place in a bowl and mix the chopped vegetables and herbs with the mustard, oil, vinegar, and salt and pepper to taste.

Cut the chicken into pieces and serve it on a platter, surrounded by the poached vegetables and the green sauce. Divide the sauce among several small bowls that you can dot around the table: the guests will definitely want to help themselves to more!

Note: If you prepare the poule au pot a day ahead, you'll be leaving the chicken and broth in the refrigerator overnight, so you can skim the fat off—it will form a hard, yellow layer of fat that is very easy to remove. The skimmed broth is absolutely delicious on its own, reheated and served before the chicken course, but you can also keep it to make a memorable risotto or tortellini al brodo.

TORTELLINI IN BROTH
CHICKEN TERRINE ASPIC WITH GREEN SAUCE

This is definitely one of the easiest and most impressive ways to transform your leftover poule au pot into an unforgettable lunch or light dinner. If you never thought that you could make a terrine, try this recipe: The hardest thing is probably deboning the leftover chicken. You will be so proud of yourself when you unmold it, and your guests will praise you: "I can't believe you know how to make a terrine!"
A cold, crisp white wine is the perfect choice to accompany this meal.

TO SERVE 6

FOR THE TORTELLINI SOUP

4 cups (1 L) homemade chicken broth

1 ¼ pounds (600 g) tortellini, with cheese or other filling

Grated Parmigiano, for serving

A few sprigs flat-leaf parsley, chopped, for garnish

Bring the broth to a boil in a pot and throw in the tortellini. Cook them until al dente, then remove the pasta with a slotted spoon, reserving the broth. Serve the pasta in soup plates, pouring the broth over each, and sprinkle with grated Parmigiano and parsley.

FOR THE TERRINE WITH GREEN SAUCE

Leftover cooked chicken from poule au pot (page 159)

1 bunch tarragon or an assortment of fresh herbs (basil, parsley, cilantro, chives)

2 packets gelatin

4 cups chicken broth (leftover chicken / vegetable broth from poule au pot) or ready made organic chicken broth

1 batch green sauce (page 160)

Pick the meat off the carcass of the chicken, remove the skin, and roughly shred the meat. Wash the tarragon, then remove the leaves and chop them. Mix the tarragon with the meat and transfer to a terrine mold, 10 inches long, 4 inches wide, and 3 inches deep. In a small saucepan over medium heat, dissolve the aspic (gelatin) in the broth. Bring to a boil, whisking constantly, and remove from the heat. Pour the liquid into the terrine, making sure that the pieces of chicken meat are completely covered. Allow to cool to room temperature, cover with plastic wrap, and then refrigerate overnight.

Note: Gelatin does not thicken until it cools.

To turn the terrine out of the mold, dip the base of the mold in hot water for a few seconds, then remove the plastic wrap and carefully turn the terrine out onto a platter. Serve with mixed green baby salad leaves and the green sauce.

HELPFUL HINT: *If a guest asks, "What can I bring?"—be specific! Tell your guest which type or brand of red or white wine or Champagne to bring, and even where to buy it if necessary. Or where to buy the dessert you would like to serve. Not only will they be contributing to the dinner—you may be helping them discover something new that they will serve at home themselves.*

ROAST LEG OF LAMB
CAULIFLOWER AND POTATO CURRY (ALOO GOBI)
RADISH SALAD

The Indian-style potato and cauliflower dish, served as an accompaniment to the leg of lamb, gives a traditional meal a new twist. And you will also be surprised by how good a simple radish salad can be. It was a classic starter in many French restaurants in the 1970s, and it goes particularly well with this meal. I like to serve everything at once, so that guests can enjoy the fresh, crunchy salad with the lamb and spiced vegetables.

TO SERVE 6

FOR THE LEG OF LAMB

1 4-pound (2 kg) leg of lamb, boned and tied (ask your butcher to do this, if you prefer)

3 garlic cloves, sliced

Salt and freshly ground black pepper

Preheat the oven to 375°F (190°C). Season all sides of the leg of lamb with salt and pepper. Using a small knife, make incisions just under ½ inch (1 cm) deep all around the leg of lamb (10 to 12 incisions). Insert a sliver of garlic into each incision. Place the leg of lamb in a roasting dish and roast for 1 hour so that the meat remains pink.

FOR THE CAULIFLOWER AND POTATO CURRY

1 head cauliflower

6 waxy potatoes (such as Yukon Golds)

2 small spring onions or 2 scallions, green included

10 sprigs cilantro

3 cloves

1 stick cinnamon

1 teaspoon cumin seeds

2 tablespoons olive oil

2 cloves garlic, minced

¾ inch (2 cm) fresh ginger, grated

1 teaspoon ground turmeric

1 teaspoon paprika

⅓ nutmeg, grated

Almonds

To save time, you might want to use garam masala, the spice mixture readily available in stores, rather than grinding the spices yourself. I'd nevertheless advise you to have these spices at hand, because they're essential for other recipes.

Clean the cauliflower and cut it into small florets. Peel the potatoes, cut them into bite-sized pieces, and rinse them. Clean and chop the onions. Wash the cilantro and chop the leaves, reserving the stalks. Set the leaves aside aside. Using a mortar and pestle, crush the cilantro stalks and grind the cardamom, cloves, cinnamon stick, and cumin seeds.

Heat the olive oil in a skillet and sauté the onions, garlic, and ginger for 2 to 3 minutes, until fragrant. Add the potato pieces and cauliflower florets and mix well. Stir in the turmeric, nutmeg, and all the ground spices until well combined. Pour in enough water to cover three-quarters of the height of the ingredients. Cover with the lid and cook over medium heat for about 10 minutes. Remove the lid and cook until almost all the liquid has evaporated and the vegetables are tender, with just a little sauce at the bottom of the skillet, about 15 to 20 minutes more. Toast the almonds in a pan without adding any fat and sprinkle them over the dish with the chopped cilantro leaves.

FOR THE RADISH SALAD

2 bunches radishes, in different colors if possible

Olive oil

Sherry vinegar

Salt and freshly ground black pepper

Wash the radishes and trim the stalks and tips. Using a mandoline, slice them into rounds. Make a classic vinaigrette, whisking together the olive oil and vinegar to form an emulsion. Dress the salad and season with salt and pepper. Serve alongside the lamb and vegetable curry.

SHEPHERD'S PIE OF CONFIT DUCK
SAUTÉED MIXED GREENS

———————————

If you want to host a weekday dinner that will not take hours to prepare and that your guests will love, this is it. Using duck confit for the filling makes this shepherd's pie sophisticated—and a cinch to prepare. Do your shopping over the weekend. If you have very little time, you can serve the duck Parmentier with a salad of mixed greens and fresh herbs.

A nice medium-bodied red wine is the perfect pairing for this comforting dinner.

TO SERVE 4

FOR THE SHEPHERD'S PIE

10 floury potatoes, such as Russets	Grated fresh nutmeg
4 confit duck legs (canned)	Salt and freshly ground black pepper
½ glass milk	2 slices melba toast
3 tablespoons (50 g) butter plus a few small knobs of butter for the top of the "pies"	1 garlic clove

Wash and peel the potatoes and cook them in a large pot of salted water. Heat the duck legs in a pan to melt the fat so that you can remove it. Debone the duck legs. Using your hands, coarsely shred the meat and set aside. When the potatoes are tender, drain them and mash them roughly with a potato masher. To make the mashed potatoes creamy, add the milk, butter, a generous sprinkling of grated nutmeg, and salt and pepper to taste. Keep potatoes warm over low heat, stirring occasionally so they do not burn.

Set the oven to broil and preheat. Rub the interiors of four individual ovenproof earthenware dishes with the garlic clove. Divide the shredded duck evenly between the four dishes, and cover with the mashed potatoes. Using the back of the tines of a fork, make lines in the mashed potato topping. Crumble the slices of melba toast with your hands, scattering the crumbs over the mashed potatoes, and dot each dish with a couple of knobs of batter. Place pies under broiler until nicely golden brown.

Note: The pies can be prepared ahead and left at room temperature. When ready to serve, place in a preheated oven at 350°F and bake for 15 minutes, then broil until top is golden.

Your guests will be delighted when you present them with individual pies, served straight from the oven.

FOR THE SAUTÉED GREENS

6 large handfuls of assorted leafy greens (spinach, Swiss chard, sugarloaf chicory, lettuce, or green cabbage leaves)

Olive oil for the skillet and for seasoning

2 garlic cloves, peeled and sliced

Salt and freshly ground black pepper

In a large pot of boiling salted water, blanch the toughest leaves (Swiss chard, cabbage leaves) for about 2 minutes, then drain in a colander and allow them to cool slightly. Heat 2 tablespoons olive oil in a skillet over medium heat. Add the sliced garlic. Add the assorted greens and sear them for 5 minutes, turning them over with a pair of tongs until they are soft and tender. Work in batches if necessary, depending on the quantity and types of leaves. Remove the pan from the heat, transfer the greens to a serving platter, and season with a little olive oil and salt and pepper.

Note: To save time, these assorted leafy greens can also be served at room temperature, seasoned simply with a drizzle of lemon juice.

MACKEREL FILLETS
MIDDLE EASTERN CARROTS
FROZEN YOGURT WITH TURKISH DELIGHT AND PISTACHIOS

———————————

Finally, mackerel is getting the recognition it deserves for its gentle flavor, flaky texture, and good-for-you omega-3 fatty acids! This is one of the best and easiest ways to prepare and enjoy it. Here, I brush it with a little harissa to add a Middle Eastern accent, and serve it with cumin-scented carrots with fresh cilantro and preserved lemon. Hummus (I buy it from my local Greek grocer) served on red endive leaves, which work as little spoons, and garnished with pomegranate seeds will make this meal a feast for the eyes as well as the palate.
For dessert, I keep with the Middle Eastern theme and serve a frozen yogurt sprinkled with crushed pistachios and small slices of loukoum, or Turkish delight.

Get into the Moroccan spirit and set a colorful table. I built my table setting around red and white plates that I picked up in Marrakech.

TO SERVE 4

FOR THE CARROTS

1 bunch carrots, about 8	**1 teaspoon cumin seeds**
1 bunch cilantro	**1 preserved lemon**
Olive oil	**1 teaspoon ground turmeric**
2 scallions, sliced	**Salt and freshly ground black pepper**
2 garlic cloves, sliced	

Peel the carrots and cut them on a diagonal into slices. Wash and chop the cilantro leaves. Heat a little olive oil in a large pot over medium high heat and sizzle the onions and garlic for a few moments. Increase the heat to high, add the carrot slices, and sweat them for 1 minute. Using a mortar and pestle, finely grind the cumin.

Remove the flesh from the preserved lemon and finely dice the skin. Add the lemon skin, cumin, and turmeric to the carrots, mixing well. Season with salt and pepper and pour in half a glass of water. Cover with the lid, reduce the heat to medium, and cook until all the liquid has been absorbed, about 15 minutes. The carrots should be firm-tender. Arrange in a serving dish and sprinkle with the chopped cilantro.

FOR THE MACKEREL

Olive oil for the baking dish

8 mackerel fillets (2 per person) — ask your fishmonger to fillet the fish

Salt

1 tablespoon harissa

1 tablespoon ground cumin

Preheat the oven to 400°F (210°C). Oil the base of an ovenproof dish and place the fillets skin side down on it. Season with salt and brush with a fine layer of harissa, then sprinkle generously with the cumin. Place dish in the upper third of the oven and broil the fillets. Keep a careful eye on them as the mackerel will cook very rapidly—the fillets should take no longer than 5 to 7 minutes.

FOR THE DESSERT

Dice some rose-scented Turkish delight, chop some pistachio nuts, and get out your Champagne saucers for serving. Scoop some vanilla frozen yogurt into each glass and garnish with the Turkish delight and pistachios.

WATERMELON, FETA, AND KALAMATA OLIVE SALAD
SAUSAGES WITH LENTILS

As soon as the weather is warm enough for watermelon to be in season, prepare this menu for your family and friends. It's easy to throw together for a large group. The sweetness of the watermelon contrasts beautifully with the salty feta, while the hearty sausages and lentils turn this into a satisfying summer meal your guests will request again and again. If you can cook the sausages on an outdoor grill, it's even better.

TO SERVE 4

FOR THE WATERMELON SALAD

1 ½ lb. watermelon	5 ounces (150 g) feta cheese
1 medium size red onion	Juice of 2 limes
15 Kalamata olives	4 tablespoons olive oil
1 bunch parsley	Salt and freshly ground black pepper
1 bunch mint	

Peel the watermelon and remove as many of the seeds as possible. Cut the flesh into bite-size cubes. Peel the red onion and thinly slice it, then soak the slices in ice water while you proceed with the rest of the preparation. This takes the edge off the taste. Remove the pits from the olives and cut each olive in half. Wash and roughly chop the parsley and mint. Drain and pat the onion slices dry.

Combine all of these ingredients in a large salad bowl and crumble the feta over the top with your hands, then gently mix.

To prepare the dressing, whisk together the lime juice, olive oil, and salt and pepper to taste. Dress the salad just before serving.

Note: Use the remaining washed mint leaves from the watermelon salad to scent a large jug of cold water for the table.

FOR THE SAUSAGES WITH LENTILS

4 Toulouse sausages or other good-quality pork sausages

5 tablespoons olive oil, plus more for cooking the sausages

14 ounces (400 g) green lentils

2 garlic cloves, peeled

1 bouquet garni (bay leaf, thyme, and rosemary)

1 yellow onion studded with 3 cloves

Sherry vinegar

A few sprigs of fresh thyme or oregano, chopped

1 red onion

20 cherry tomatoes

Salt and freshly ground black pepper

Preheat the oven to 400°F (210°C). Brush the sausages with oil, place them on a rimmed baking sheet or in an ovenproof dish and cook for 20 minutes, until browned and cooked through.

Pour the lentils into a pot and add enough cold water to cover them. I usually add 2 cups of water to 1 cup lentils. Add the garlic cloves, bouquet garni, and onion. Bring to a simmer and cook over low heat for 20 minutes, checking occasionally to make sure there is sufficient water to cook the lentils properly. When they are done (lentils will be tender but will retain their shape), remove the bouquet garni and onion.

Using a slotted spoon, transfer the cooked lentils to the serving dish. Salt and pepper to taste. Crush the garlic cloves with the back of a spoon and stir the pulp into the lentils. Stir in 5 tablespoons of olive oil and 1 to 2 tablespoons of sherry vinegar. Sprinkle with the chopped thyme. Allow to cool to lukewarm. Halve the cherry tomatoes and finely slice the red onion. Stir into the lentil salad. Taste for salt and pepper.

Note: If you are lucky enough to find Italian fennel-scented sausages, the dish will be even better. But there's another solution: If you get on well with your butcher and plan on making this dish for a large number of guests, ask him to prepare the sausages with fennel seeds, which you can offer to provide.

MY GRANDMOTHER'S BRAISED RABBIT
POLENTA FRIES
BAKED APPLES

I can always count on this recipe to make everyone ooh and ahhh. I have even made it for Venetians
at my friend's palazzo for a very chic yet casual lunch.
Yes, I really did learn this recipe from my grandmother, and it is easy and so delicious! Even those who normally
shy away from rabbit will be dipping their polenta fries in the sauce.

TO SERVE 6

FOR THE BRAISED RABBIT

3 yellow onions

Olive oil

2 sprigs rosemary

1 bunch sage, leaves picked

3 saddles of rabbit, halved

3 rabbit hind legs and thighs, left whole

¾ cup (200 ml) white wine

8 ounces (250 g) peeled canned whole tomatoes, mashed slightly by hand

1 tablespoon tomato paste

Salt and freshly ground black pepper

Chop the onions. Heat a little olive oil in a large cast-iron pot over high heat and sizzle the onions with the sprigs of rosemary and a few sage leaves (set the remaining leaves aside for the polenta fries). Push the onions to the sides of the pot, add the pieces of rabbit, and cook on both sides until nicely golden. (If the pot is not large enough, work in two batches.) Allow the chopped onions to caramelize, taking care not to burn them. Deglaze with the white wine and simmer for 3 to -4 minutes to allow the alcohol to evaporate. If necessary, and you have removed the meat from the pot, return all the pieces of meat to the pot. Add the canned peeled tomatoes and stir in the tomato paste, mixing well. Season with salt and pepper. Cover with the lid, reduce the heat to very low, and allow to simmer gently for about 1 hour. Keep an eye on the amount of sauce in the pan, as you may need to add a little water to dilute it.

I like to bring the cast iron pot to the table (making sure to wipe off any drippings on the outside of the pan), set it on a trivet, and serve each guest. They can help themselves to seconds!

FOR THE POLENTA FRIES

6 cups (1.5 liters) water

Salt for the water

14 ounces (400 g) instant cornmeal

Olive oil

Fresh sage leaves for garnish

While the rabbit is cooking, bring salted water to a boil. Pour in the cornmeal, stirring with a whisk to prevent lumps from forming. Reduce the heat to low and continue stirring for about 5 minutes. Remove from the heat. Oil a 9-inch by 13-inch baking dish and pour the hot polenta into it, smoothing it to make a layer ¾-inch (2-cm) thick. Allow to cool for 1 hour, until firmed up.

Set the oven to broil and preheat. Cut the polenta into strips ¾ inch (2 cm) wide and then into fries about 2 inches (5 cm) long. With a brush, lightly oil the polenta strips and place them under the broiler until nicely golden. Drizzle a little olive oil into a skillet (just enough to cover the base) and fry the sage leaves until crisp. Place the polenta fries on a serving platter and scatter with the fried sage leaves.

FOR THE BAKED APPLES

6 Boskoop apples or other baking apples of about the same size

6 brown sugar cubes or 6 teaspoons brown sugar

Ground cinnamon

6 knobs butter

Vanilla ice cream as an accompaniment

Preheat the oven to 350°F (180°F). Wash, peel, and core the apples. Place them in an ovenproof dish (they should fit snugly) and prick them here and there so they don't burst as they cook. In the hollow of each apple, place a sugar cube and a knob of butter. Sprinkle with cinnamon and pour a little water into the bottom of the dish.

Bake until tender, about 30 minutes, depending on the size of the apples. Allow to cool slightly and serve warm with a scoop of vanilla ice cream.

MUSSELS WITH SEMOLINA
SCENTED WITH GARLIC, GINGER, AND CILANTRO

———————————

Since this menu comprises a one-pot dish featuring mussels, I suggest you serve a starter based on seafood as well: Salmon roe and tarama spread on thin Norwegian cracker bread makes a good foil for the main dish, which is more exotic, with its mix of spices and couscous. Pair this predinner snack with a cocktail of iced Champagne, elderberry syrup, and lemon zest (a cocktail usually known as a Hugo) to set a refined tone for the evening.

TO SERVE 4

6 pounds (3 kg) mussels, preferably large

10 ounces (300 g) precooked semolina (couscous)

3 garlic cloves

1 tablespoon freshly grated ginger

6 tablespoons (100 g) softened butter

1 large glass boiling water

3 sticks lemon grass, cut into small pieces

1 bunch cilantro, chopped

2 limes, quartered

Preheat the oven to 375°F (190°C). Wash, scrub, and rinse the mussels.

Spread the semolina out in an ovenproof dish. Crush and peel the garlic cloves and combine them with the ginger and softened butter in a glass. Stir in an equal amount of boiling water until well combined and pour the mixture evenly over the semolina.

Place the prepared mussels in a large pot over high heat and add the lemon grass. Cover with the lid and cook for at least 10 minutes, or until the mussels open. You do not need to add any water to the mussels as they will produce their own broth. Remove from the heat and allow to cool enough to handle. Remove and discard any mussels that have not opened, as they should not be eaten.

Evenly pour 2 ladlefuls of the mussel cooking juices over the semolina so that it plumps up, and then separate the grains using a fork. Arrange the mussels over the semolina. Cover the dish with a sheet of foil to prevent the mussels from drying out and put the dish in the oven to reheat for about 10 minutes. Scatter the chopped cilantro over the mussels and couscous and serve with the lime wedges.

When you set the table, don't forget to provide small bowls of warm water with lemon juice so that guests can rinse their fingers, as well as small individual plates or small bowls for the empty mussel shells.

BABY SPINACH SALAD WITH POMEGRANATE SEEDS
SLOW COOKED AND ROASTED LEMON AND GARLIC CHICKEN
BULGUR WITH CILANTRO

This is an easy weekend dinner that will allow you to enjoy the company of your guests and inspire them to ask for the recipes! I have tasted different variations of this chicken dish in Sicily, Greece, and the South of France. Seek out the best organic lemons possible: when they are cooked and slightly caramelized, their quality will shine through.

TO SERVE 4 TO 6

FOR THE BABY SPINACH SALAD

1¼ pounds (600 g) baby spinach leaves

Juice of 1 lemon

Olive oil

Salt and freshly ground black pepper

1 espresso cup sliced almonds

Seeds of ½ a pomegranate
Note: can substitute with ¾ cup dried cranberries

Wash and dry the baby spinach leaves and place them in a salad bowl. Prepare a dressing, whisking together the lemon juice, olive oil as needed, and salt and pepper to taste to form an emulsion.

Roast the almonds in a skillet without adding any fat or toast them briefly under a preheated broiler, keeping a careful eye on them to make sure they don't burn. Scatter the roasted almonds and pomegranate seeds over the spinach, pour the dressing on top, and toss just before serving.

FOR THE CHICKEN

1 free-range chicken, cut into 8 pieces

1 head garlic, divided into cloves, unpeeled

2 unwaxed or organic lemons, cut into eight to ten pieces

1 small handful fresh thyme leaves (you may

also use fresh rosemary or oregano)

¼ cup (60 ml) olive oil

1 small glass white wine

Salt and freshly ground black pepper

Preheat the oven to 325°F (160°C). Place the chicken pieces in an ovenproof dish with the garlic gloves, lemon pieces, and thyme. Drizzle with the olive oil and mix well using your hands, leaving the chicken pieces skin side up. Pour the white wine over the top and season with salt and pepper. Cover tightly with a double sheet of foil to keep the moisture in. Roast for 1½ hours to allow the flavors to penetrate the chicken meat. Remove the foil and roast for an additional 20 minutes, or until the chicken skin is crisp and golden and the lemon quarters are caramelized.

FOR THE BULGUR WITH CILANTRO

1 cup bulgur

A few sprigs cilantro

3 scallions

3 tablespoons olive oil

Salt and freshly ground black pepper

Rinse the bulgur in cold water. Place in a heatproof mixing bowl and cover with boiling water. Cover the bowl with aluminum foil and Let sit for about 15 minutes, allowing the grains to plump up, adding more boiling water if they remain too crunchy. While you wait, chop the cilantro and wash and finely chop the onions scallions. Drain the bulgur in a colander. Place all the ingredients in a serving dish, adding the olive oil and salt and pepper to taste. Toss until well combined. Keep warm.

Just before serving, spoon the chicken cooking juices over the bulgur.

HELPFUL HINT: *Be sure to have at least 10 of your favorite color cotton napkins. You can always find them on sale and they make a difference in making your family and guests feel special.*

MERCEDES CHILI BEANS
GUACAMOLE
MARGARITAS

A friend's mother taught him this recipe for a homemade chili that can be easily adapted for six, eight, or twenty-five people. I have made this recipe for over twenty years and found that a good lean ground beef works best here. I like to use a mix of pinto beans and red beans because cooked red beans are more firm while the pinto beans add an earthier flavor. Soaking your beans for at least two hours ahead of time will shorten the cooking time and keep the beans from breaking apart, as long as you do not cook them on a high boil. You need time to put this meal together, but it is easier than it looks and everyone will be so happy that they were on your guest list!

Get into the party spirit with your table setting and make sure your margaritas are ice cold! I like providing at least two small bowls of tortillas chips or two baskets of corn tortillas, distributed around the table.

TO SERVE 8

1 lb (500 g) mixed dry beans: half pinto beans and half red kidney beans	Salt
3 cloves garlic, cut in half	

FOR THE MEAT AND CHILI MIXTURE:

2 tablespoons New Mexico chili powder	4 cloves garlic, finely chopped
2 tablespoons California chili powder	2¼ lbs (1 kg) lean ground beef
3 dried whole California chiles	Salt
3 dried whole New Mexico chiles	

To cook the beans, first sort them to remove any rocks or visible pieces of dirt. I also remove any broken beans. Rinse the beans in cold water in a colander and put them in a large pan or bowl of cold tap water to soak for at least 2 hours, or overnight. Water should be 1 inch above the beans.

When you are ready to cook the beans, drain and rinse them. Put the beans in a large pan (you will add the chile mix to the same pan, so be sure it is big enough) and cover with enough cold tap water to cover the beans by about 3 inches (7.5 cm). Add the halved garlic cloves. Cover the pot and bring to a medium boil, then reduce heat to a soft boil.

After 40 minutes, add 4 teaspoons of salt to the pot and continue to cook until the beans are al dente but not soft, since they will cook more when the chile mixture is added.

Remove and set aside most of the cooking liquid from the beans so that the liquid in the pot comes just 1 inch above the beans.

To cook the chiles: Rinse the whole dried chiles in warm tap water. Put the chiles in a saucepan large enough to hold them without breaking them. Cover with cold tap water and bring to a boil, then cook for at least 1 ½ hours on a low simmer.

When the chiles are soft, carefully take them out of the cooking water, remove the stems, and put them in a blender. Reserve 2 cups of the chile cooking water. Blend the chiles just long enough for them to become a thick chili sauce. Set aside.

Note: You can prepare the chili sauce the day before the party; keep it in the refrigerator until you are ready to cook the beans.

To brown and season the ground beef: Brown the meat in two batches so that it browns faster and easier. In a large skillet, heat 2 tablespoons of the olive oil until the skillet is hot enough to cook the garlic without browning it. After 3 or 4 minutes, add the meat, and sprinkle 1 tablespoon each of the California and New Mexico chile powder over it. Turn up the heat and cook until the meat browns slightly, about 12 to 15 minutes, adding 1 teaspoon of salt after 5 minutes of cooking. Use a wooden spoon to break up the meat and mix in the chile powder.

When the meat is browned, add it to the pan with the cooked beans and mix them together using a wooden spoon so you do not break too many beans. Add 4 tablespoons of the reserved chili sauce to the meat and beans and mix it in with the wooden spoon. (This is why I told you to cook the beans in a pan that was large enough to hold the seasoned meat!)

Put the chili beans over a medium heat making sure that you gently stir the stew while it is heating so that it does not stick to the bottom of your pan. When the chili beans begin to bubble, lower the heat so that they are cooking slowly, cover the pot, and cook for 1 ½ hours. If you need to add more liquid, alternate between the cooking liquid from the beans and the red chile juice that you set aside. When the chili is done cooking, check for salt and spiciness, adding chili sauce and powdered chili to taste. Serve with the garnish and guacamole.

FOR THE CHILI BEAN GARNISH

1 bunch cilantro, leaves separated from stems

1 cup green onions or scallions, washed, dried, and finely chopped

1½ cups Manchego cheese, grated on

larger holes of grater

1½ cups Cheddar cheese, grated on larger holes of grater

1½ cups sour cream

Wash, dry, and roughly chopped the cilantro leaves. (You can chop the stems finely and use in them in the guacamole recipe, below.) Mix the chopped cilantro and green onions with both cheeses and refrigerate until serving.

FOR THE GUACAMOLE

7 ripe avocados

20 cherry tomatoes, washed and diced, reserved with their tomato juice

½ fresh red bell pepper, washed, seeded, and cut into small dice

½ fresh yellow or orange bell pepper, washed, seeded, and cut into small dice

½ bunch cilantro, washed, dried, and chopped, not too finely

3 spring onions with the greens, washed,

dried and finely chopped, or ¼ cup of finely chopped scallions

½ clove of garlic, finely chopped

Juice of ½ an organic lemon or lime

½ teaspoon sea salt

¼ of a fresh, seeded jalapeño pepper, finely chopped

Tortilla chips or warm corn tortillas, for serving

Peel and remove pits from the avocados. Using a large fork or a potato masher, mash the avocados in a large wooden or glass bowl until fairly smooth but not a "puree." A few bits of unmashed avocado are always nice. Add the tomatoes, bell peppers, onions, and garlic and gently mix using a large wooden spoon. Add the cilantro and lemon (or lime) juice and gently mix. Mix in the jalapeno and salt. Taste and adjust for salt and "heat."

Note: I like freshly made guacamole, so prefer to make it no more than 1 hour ahead. If you do make ahead, put 2 avocado pits on top of the guacamole and drizzle with fresh lemon juice to prevent it from turning brown. Cover with plastic wrap and refrigerate. Be sure to remove from the refrigerator 30 minutes before serving.

Remove pits and stir in lemon juice before serving, with tortilla chips or warm corn tortillas.

FOR CLASSIC MARGARITAS

8 oz. fresh squeezed lime juice

8 oz. Cointreau

16 oz. good-quality tequila

Splash of fresh-squeezed orange juice

Shake or stir the ingredients. Serve over crushed ice or on the rocks, garnished with a half a lime or an orange slice.

BREKFAST

Having guests for breakfast is a great way to spend time with family and friends. Of course, you'll have to do your shopping ahead of time, and go to bed early. If you don't have time to buy freshly baked bread at the bakery just beforehand, ask your guests to bring over all the baked goods you'll need.

Make sure the table is festively set. Besides serving the classic morning drinks—tea, coffee, and fresh-squeezed juices—prepare a few unusual dishes, such as: orange salad sprinkled with mint and chopped pistachios, individual servings of ricotta cheese drizzled with honey, and brioches filled with pistachio ice cream——sure to be a hit with all ages! I got this idea in Sicily recently, where I learned that part of the morning meal is a toasted almond granita served with a brioche. Delicioso!

A PAIR OF CEVICHES
SLOW-COOKED BONITO SALAD WITH WHITE BEANS
MIMOSA COCKTAILS

All of us are ready for spring after a long, cold winter. When the first days of sunshine come along, I always like to mark the occasion by getting my friends together for a celebratory luncheon. Start with a take on the classic mimosa using grapefruit syrup and prosecco. A couple of Peruvian-inspired ceviches and a white bean and bonito salad make for a delicious lunch that will put guests in a good mood, knowing that more sunny days are ahead!

TO SERVE 30

FOR THE MIMOSA COCKTAILS

I use a container that is large enough (or 2 glass pitchers) to hold the juice of six oranges combined with 4 ounces of grapefruit syrup and three bottles of prosecco. Serve this beautifully hued cocktail in large glasses with ice cubes.

FOR THE POLLACK CEVICHE WITH SWEET POTATOES

2¼ pounds (1 kg) sweet potatoes	2 bunches pink radishes
4½ pounds (2 kg) yellow pollack fillets, skinned	10 limes
3 red onions	⅔ cup Olive oil for the marinade
1 jalapeno pepper	Fleur de sel
2 bunches cilantro	7 ounces (200 g) roasted, salted corn kernels

Rinse the sweet potatoes, place them in a large pot, and cover them with water. Bring to a boil and cook for 15 to 20 minutes. Check for doneness with the tip of a knife: they should remain al dente. Rinse them under cold water and allow them to cool to room temperature. Remove the skins and cut the sweet potatoes into approximately 1-inch (2-cm) cubes.

Cut the fish fillets into cubes of the same size as the sweet potatoes. Finely chop the onions. Split the chili pepper in two and remove the seeds and white ribs, then finely dice the flesh. Wash and chop the cilantro. Wash the radishes and use a mandolin to slice them finely. Juice the limes.

Place the fish cubes in a large mixing bowl and add the chili pepper, fleur de sel, ⅔ cup of olive oil, and three-quarters of the lime juice. Stir well to combine, cover with plastic wrap, and place in the refrigerator to chill for at least 1 hour to cook the fish.

Arrange the sweet potato cubes with the onions, corn kernels, cilantro, and radish slices in a single dish or several dishes. Drain the marinade from the cubes of fish and add them to the dish. Carefully stir to combine and pour in the remaining lime juice. Adjust the seasoning, generously pouring in more olive oil if necessary. Serve well chilled.

FOR THE PRAWN , AVOCADO, AND GRAPEFRUIT CEVICHE

6 pink grapefruit	**Fleur de sel**
60 jumbo shrimp (2 per person)	**Olive oil**
6 avocados	**Crushed ground chili pepper**
1 bunch chives	**7 ounces (200 g) fresh shelled peas**

Carefully peel the grapefruit, removing all of the white pith. Working over a bowl to catch the juice (that you'll need for the seasoning), remove the segments from between the membranes.

Throw the shrimp into a pot of boiling water and cook them for 2 minutes. Drain them and allow to cool. Shell them and cut them into halves lengthwise, removing the black vein.

Peel and dice the avocados. Wash and chop the chives.

Combine the grapefruit juice with the salt, olive oil, and chili pepper to taste to make the dressing.

Transfer all of the ingredients to a serving dish, add the dressing and gently combine. Taste and add some of the reserved grapefruit juice if necessary.

You can make this 1 hour ahead and keep refrigerated until ready to serve.

SLOW-COOKED BONITO SALAD WITH WHITE BEANS

3 pounds (1.5 kg) bonito fillets

3 cloves garlic, peeled and halved

1 sprig rosemary

4 cups (1 liter) olive oil

4 pounds (2 kg) dry white beans

3 cloves garlic

1 pomegranate

1 pound (500 g) arugula

White wine vinegar

Fleur de sel and freshly ground black pepper

I always prepare more fillets than the quantity immediately required for this recipe. They keep very well in their oil, and they are delicious used instead of canned tuna to make a Niçoise salad (see recipe, page 126). Having said that, if you're pressed for time, or can't find fresh bonito to make this recipe, good-quality canned tuna will do just as well.

Bonita is another delicious, overlooked fish that is best prepared simply.
Even though this recipes calls for the fish to rest and "cook" in olive oil, it does not absorb the oil because of the low "cooking" temperature and the density of the fish.

Arrange the fish fillets in a Dutch oven or large pot with the garlic halves and rosemary. Pour in the olive oil; the ingredients should be covered. Gently heat the pot until it is a little warmer than lukewarm—check by carefully dipping in a finger. (If you have a kitchen thermometer, the temperature should be between 104 and 122°F / 40 and 50°C). Cover the pot, remove it from the heat, and allow the fish to cook gently for about 30 minutes. It should give a little when touched.

If you are going to be preparing a larger quantity and your pot is not big enough, work in two batches, reusing the oil.

To prepare the beans, see the recipe on page 109. Reserve the garlic cloves that have cooked with the haricot beans and crush them to add to the salad vinaigrette (see below). Cooking rids them of their strong taste and they will bring a delicate flavor to the seasoning.

For the vinaigrette: Whisk together the vinegar, cooked garlic, olive oil, and salt and pepper to taste to make an emulsion.

Seed the pomegranate, taking care to eliminate all of the white membranes.
Arrange a bed of arugula on a large platter and spread the haricot beans over it. In the center, place the pieces of bonito.
Sprinkle attractively with the pomegranate seeds. Season with salt and pepper and drizzle generously with the vinaigrette.

For dessert, pass round macarons in spring-colored hues to match your lunch!

CHRISTMAS TIME PARTY: FOIE GRAS ON ENDIVE LEAVES
OYSTERS ON THE HALF SHELL
LENTILS WITH GRILLED SAUSAGES

Let's be honest. Christmas entertaining can be either fun or terribly stressful!

Remember rule number one: Give yourself enough prep time! Do not over extend yourself, and serve food that will not have you slaving over the stove or be too complicated. A great presentation makes everything taste better and makes your guests feel special.

The chilled champagne is flowing and the menu, of course, features the Christmas Eve classics. Depending on how many guests you have, you might need some help:

Scenario 1: A good friend will be opening the oysters, but he or she won't be having much fun that evening.

Scenario 2: You hire staff for the evening. After they have opened the oysters, they'll help you serve the guests.

TO SERVE 20

2 whole semi-cooked foie gras (mi-cuits)

2¼ pounds (1 kg) red Belgian endives

1 jar store-bought red berry jelly (cranberry, red currant, blackberry)

Oysters of your choice (an average of 6 per person)

1 pomegranate

FOR THE PLATTERS OF FOIE GRAS

Arrange similarly sized red Belgian endive leaves to form a star on a large platter. Place a generous helping of foie gras in each leaf and top with a teaspoon of the jelly.

FOR THE PLATTERS OF OYSTERS

Make a bed of coarse salt to ensure that the opened shells are stable. A pomegranate "bead"' adds a festive touch (and its acidity is a great replacement for that of the classic lemon).

Don't forget to ask your designated oyster shucker to detach the oyster from its base while he's opening them. Most of your guests will be standing when the oysters are served and this make it easier to enjoy this oh-so-delicate shellfish. As a main course, I like to serve my sausages with lentils in individual bowls, which also makes it easy to serve this part of the meal.

For the ingredients and instructions for this dish, see page 184. On such occasions, I ask my butcher to prepare, especially for me, the now well-known sausage with fennel seeds!

FOR THE LENTILS WITH GRILLED SAUSAGES (SEE PAGE 184)

Fill the bowls with hot lentils and add a serving of sausage on a wooden skewer. At the end of the year, lentils are traditionally synonymous with prosperity. I learned about the wonderful surf-and-turf combination of oysters and sausages from friends in the Bordeaux region.

FOR DESSSERT

To end on a sweet note, serve a scoop of lemon sorbet doused in vodka, or sweet treats such as marrons glacés (candied chestnuts), fruit jellies, or chocolates.

As a final—and thoughtful—touch when your guests are departing, hand them a generous portion of the giant panettone that has served as a centerpiece at the table. Wrap each piece in a cloth bag tied with a ribbon of your choice. When they sit down for a late breakfast next morning, they can munch on slices of toasted panettone, reminiscing about the lovely evening spent in your company.

ACKNOWLEDGMENTS

I would like to express my special thanks to Sofia Coppola, who had the idea and inspiration for me to write *Dîner à la Maison*, and who has supported me at every step of the book's journey.

My gratitude and great thanks go to Robert, for his unconditional love and strength, which upheld me throughout. His innate creativity and force of life are a constant inspiration to me.

Huge thanks to my dearest friends Phiphi, Florence, Cédric, Elena, and Géraldine, who generously lent me dinnerware, cutlery, tablecloths, and napkins to mix in with my own collection.

Thank you Frédéric, who helped me with creative graphics, and to Alicia, who helped me with some of the words.

Big thanks to my dearest sister, Emmanuelle, who spent many hours transcribing the manuscript from my phone and correcting my grammar on the way.

It has been a great pleasure to work with a fantastic team at Rizzoli. Thank you to Charles Miers and Jacob Lehman.

Thank you to Joseph Logan and Anamaria Morris for your art direction and innate understanding of what I wanted for this book.

I am a lucky man.

CREDITS

Flatware pp. 8, 51, 52, 53, 138, 139, 159, 160, 161, 178, 179, 181 from the Marly collection by Christofle.

Placemats pp. 10, 26, 27, 35, 43, 56, and 57 by MY DRAP.

Stainless steel bowl pp. 19, 51, 52; wooden spatula p. 58; small glass on p. 84; stainless steel platters pp. 138, 159, 175; glass p. 154; and slotted spoon p. 192 reproduced with kind permission of Alessi.

Bucky Champagne bucket, Champagne Tulip glasses, and wine and water Tulip goblets pp. 19, 51, 52, 149, 150, 151, 173, 175, 181, 194, 218, 221 reproduced with the kind permission of Paola C. srl., Italy.

Arne Jacobsen cutlery in stainless steel (1957) from Georg Jensen appears pp. 19, 27, 35, 87 (knife and fork); pp. 20, 26, 36, 62, 72, 112, 178, 186, 202 (spoons); 71, 80, 154, 192, 214 (forks); and p. 107 (knife, fork, and spoon).

Salt and pepper set (pp. 19, 185), AJ water pitcher (p. 38), sugar bowl (p. 71), stainless serving platter (pp. 71, 210), Freja water pitcher (pp. 150, 180), and ashtray (p. 216) reproduced with kind permission of Stelton A/S, www.stelton.com.

White porcelain plates pp. 19, 43, 60, and 61 courtesy of Rosenthal GmbH.

Kitchen knife pp. 20, 24, 32, 36, 54, 112, 170, 176; sake glasses p. 65; perforated tongs p. 104; casserole (Nambu Iron Stewpot) pp. 146, 148, 151, 189; and serving utensils p. 214 reproduced with kind permission of Yanagi shop, Japan.

Pepper mill pp. 20, 24, 40, 56, 79, 84, and 102 courtesy of Adhoc Design Shop.

Flatware pp. 23, 30, 31, 43, 56, 57, 83, 91, 93, 96, 97, 101, 102, 103, 118, 119, 122, 126, 127, 129, 130, 132, 133, 143, 144, 145, 205 (teaspoon), 208, and 209 (teaspoons, forks, and knives) courtesy Robert Welch Designs Limited.

Beige plates pp. 23, 38, 39, 114, 137, and 139 courtesy of Merci.

Pepper mill pp. 28, 54, 58, 66, 72, 76, 88, 98, 116, 148, 196; and salt and pepper mills p. 140 courtesy of Peugeot France.

Alpha water tumbler pp. 35, 51, 52, 70, 87, 149, 150, 151, 159, 160, 162, 165, 173, 175, 178, 179, 185, 186, 189, 218, and 221; alpha water pitcher p. 169; and wine glass 267 pp. 70, 159, 160, 178, 179, 181 courtesy of J. & L. Lobmeyr.

Margherite Daisy glass pp. 31 and 61 reproduced with kind permission of Laguna B., Venice, Italy.

The Bleu du Four dinner plates pp. 35, 107, 108, 198, 199, and 201 have been reproduced with the kind permission of Site Corot Limoges Porcelain.

White ceramic serving dishes pp. 36 and 57 from Eva Trio by Ole Palsby.

Serving bowls pp. 38 and 39 courtesy of Tse & Tsé Associés.

Micro-grater pp. 54, 170, and 192 by Microplane.

Plates pp. 56, 57; porcelain bowls p. 71; porcelain and rectangular plates p. 87 by Hakusan, Japan.

Bowls p. 83 courtesy of Ceramiche de Simone, srl.

Blue-and-white dinner plates pp. 114, 115, 137, and 138 courtesy of Nicola Fasano.

Casseroles pp. 116, 123, 186, 192, 205 courtesy of Le Creuset France.

Knife p. 141 by Calmels Laguiole.

Flatware pp. 8, 173 (serving spoon and fork), 175 (fork), 185 from the Chinon collection by Christofle.

Painting p. 178 by Eric Baudart.

Porcelain platter pp. 178, 181, 217, and 220 reproduced with kind permission of Jasper Morrison.

Garlic press p. 192 by OXO.

Cocktail cart p. 194 reproduced with kind permission of USM U Schärer fils sa.

Artwork p. 216 by Lionel Esteve.

Mirror p. 218 reproduced with kind permission of Pierre Charpin.

Silver champagne goblets pp. 218, 220, and 221 courtesy of Puiforcat.

First published in the United States of America in 2019 by
Rizzoli International Publications, Inc.
300 Park Avenue South
New York, NY 10010
www.rizzoliusa.com

Compilation and texts © 2019 Laurent Buttazzoni

Introduction © 2019 Sofia Coppola

Photography © 2019 Charlotte Hess

Design by Joseph Logan, assisted by Anamaria Morris

ISBN: 978-0-8478-6470-6
Library of Congress Catalog Control Number: 2019930324

2019 2020 2021 2022 / 10 9 8 7 6 5 4 3 2 1

Printed in Italy